GREAT GOLF COURSES OF THE WORLD

•

GREAT GOLF COURSES OF THE WORLD

•

BY ANDRÉ-JEAN LAFAURIE

PHOTOGRAPHS BY JEAN-FRANÇOIS LEFÈVRE

FOREWORD BY JOHN GARRITY, *SPORTS ILLUSTRATED*

ARTABRAS, A DIVISION OF ABBEVILLE PRESS

PUBLISHERS

NEW YORK · LONDON · PARIS

ACKNOWLEDGMENTS

The author and editor would like to thank the following: Nicole Mahé and Air France; Golf Travel; the Austrian and Irish offices of tourism; the Byblos Andaluz hotel in Mijas, Spain; the Casa de Campo Resort in Santo Domingo, Dominican Republic; the directors of each golf course; Saab France; and Maureen Lefèvre.

Translation by Trish Valicenti
Photographs of Augusta National Course by Didier Chicot
Jacket design by Julie Rauer

JACKET FRONT: Casa de Campo, Dominican Republic
JACKET BACK: Desert Highlands, Scottsdale, Arizona

Library of Congress Cataloging-in-Publication Data

Lafaurie, André-Jean.
  Golf : great courses of the world / by André-Jean Lafaurie ; photographs by Jean-François Lefèvre.
    p. cm.
  ISBN 0-89660-016-5
  1. Golf courses.   I. Title.
GV975.L34 1991
796.352'06'8—dc20   90-46865
                                               CIP

CONTENTS

FOREWORD

"Are those mosquitoes dangerous?" a wary Sam Snead once asked a hotel manager in the Belgian Congo.

"Not if you've had spotted fever, malaria, and dengue fever," came the reply.

Forty years later, the globetrotting golfer faces few such perils. The tee markers are out from Azerbaijan to Zambia. It's not unusual for today's American tournament pro to have played either the Asian or European tours before earning his PGA Tour card, and most of the top money winners have cashed prize checks on three or more continents. At this writing, golf course construction is booming in Singapore, business tycoons are driving balls off mountain tops in Japan, and men in fur hats are prac-

ticing sand shots in Moscow. Planning a trip? Your travel agent can book you on five Irish golf courses in five days or send you to Africa to find out which is scarier—a charging rhino in Kenya or a downhill five-footer in Morocco.

Not surprisingly, the one hole on a great golf course that used to be known as its "signature hole"—usually a par 3 with an Amazon rain forest on the left, the Grand Canyon on the right, Vesuvius behind, and 228 yards of boiling surf to carry—is now commonly called the "postcard hole." More shots have been taken at the sixteenth at Cypress Point with Canons and Nikes than were ever made with MacGregors and Pings, and it's the rare golfer

who doesn't own at least one book filled with beautiful pictures of Mauna Kea, Pebble Beach, Saint Andrews, and Augusta. One even hears the complaint that golf architects intentionally sacrifice playability for photographability. The English Walker Cup golfer of the 1920s, Eustace Storey, reportedly took one look from the second tee at the Pine Valley Golf Club and said, "Tell me, do you chaps actually play this hole—or just photograph it?"

Good question. You can't do both well—that is, play golf and take pictures at the same time. Having played several of the courses within these covers, I can testify that the challenge of the game—not to mention the necessity of maintaining one's end of the conversation with one's golfing companions—distracts mightily from the scenery. The grandeur is glimpsed, so to speak, but never assimilated.

Similarly, giving the spectacular sights their due detracts from the golf and slows play to a crawl. A member of my foursome paused to take photos on the eighteenth tee at Pebble Beach a couple of years ago, drawing angry rebukes from the golfers behind us. This so afflicted my concentration that I hooked more balls into the ocean than usual.

The truth is, both good writing and good photography demand the same singleness of purpose as low-handicap golf. Golf course photographers do their best work on the borders of dusk and dawn and say it's because the light is best then. I suspect it's also because few golfers are about at those hours to impair the view and dull the senses with their buffoonery.

Preternatural patience also helps. At Saint Andrews, I once found *Sports Illustrated* photographer Lane Stewart sitting with his feet dangling in the Swilcan Burn, his reflex camera aimed at the gray clubhouse of the Royal and Ancient Golf Club. It was two hours before sunset on a wet, overcast day, but Lane thought there was a one in twenty chance the sun might break through. "I'll be ready if it does," he said.

The same patience shows in the text provided here by the French author André-Jean Lafaurie, who obviously spent as many hours pondering these courses as he did playing them. His well-aimed mix of golf history, architectural theory, and aesthetics lands somewhere between travel writing and art criticism, but the player's point of view is never more than a short chip away. The author obviously shares my own conviction that the most sublime golf is solitary golf, as when he describes the inland golf course as "a landscape on which one of the ceaseless quests of the golfer is within reach from the first shot: isolation."

Perhaps it was that quest that led the author off the well-trod path of previous golf course books. The old warhorses are here, to be sure—Saint Andrews, Ballybunion, Augusta, Pebble, and Cypress—but Lafaurie and photographer Jean-François Lefèvre take us, as well, to Skellefteå in Sweden, near the arctic circle, where one can book a 1 a.m. tee time; to Egypt, where golfers play in the shadow of the Giza Pyramids; and to the chateau at Ravenstein, where the royal family of Belgium holds court. And on: to Martinique, to the Ivory Coast, to the Arizona desert. And on: to the German forests, to the suburbs of Lisbon, to the warm-water island capital of Santo Domingo.

The only danger to the reader is that exposure to these golf courses may inspire uncontrollable wanderlust. Turning these pages, I felt an urgent impulse to return to Kashmir, in northern India, where I once spent a night in a former raj's palace on the shore of beautiful Lake Dal. There was a golf course between the palace and the

water, and I remember standing in the road shortly after sunrise, peering at the course through the trees and vines. A well-fed man in an expensive golf sweater and a turban putted while a caddie in khakis held the flag.

I can't explain why, but that moment is indelible in my memory. Similar moments await you, I am sure, in the pages that follow. Stand on tiptoe if necessary, find the best view through the trees and vines ... and, please, pay attention to your guides.

A world of golf awaits you.

John Garrity,
Sports Illustrated

7

THE GREAT GREEN THEATER

The game of golf was never invented, nor was its architecture. They were both discovered over time.

In the quest for new arenas of play it is rare that a course proves to be both beautiful and challenging. While universally acceptable criteria can be found to determine whether or not a golf course is technically adequate, no criteria on earth can technically classify its beauty. Personal taste is the sole barometer; you like or do not like a course. You can explain your particular preference, and golfers are certainly not shy about doing so. But you cannot prove that you're right or wrong.

Who is the ultimate judge of a course's design? The average golfer. Average does not mean mediocre; this golfer is average because he is placed between the extremes. As such he is necessarily on another level from the player for whom the golf course is ultimately conceived, the champion. Herein lies the ambiguity of the golf course; if it were suitable for the average golfer, the game would collapse. A course is sustained by the great number, but conceived for the few who can test its limits.

The word "golf" dates back to the fifteenth century, and the game's roots probably go back even further; its primitive ancestor was played on the flat land of the Netherlands before making its way to Scotland. As long as the game of golf was played without rules, the Scottish courses were merely converted moors. The earliest golfers had neither the technical means nor the audacity to reconstruct nature. The second age of the golf course, one that we might even call the first for "golf architecture," began around 1850, when the first courses were actually *constructed*—that is, built to a design. This second period lasted until about 1900, a half-century that sufficed to dye the entire planet green with lawns—not a single continent was spared. But until the end of the 1910s golf landscaping stagnated; the original concepts were simply

perpetuated. The twenties have been termed the Golden Age of Golf Course Architecture in America, with the most important activity coming from Pennsylvania. This period gave rise to architects such as A.W. Tillinghast, George Crump, George C. Thomas, Jr., and William S. Flynn, and also brought great advancements in course style and originality. The 1930s ushered in the "American architecture" originated by Robert Trent-Jones, which endures to this day. Nevertheless few courses were built after World War II. The golf world had to await the arrival of a golf and media genius, Arnold Palmer, toward the end of the 1950s for the game to take off again.

The resulting proliferation was daunting. For a time the era of penal architecture prevailed, devoted to traps, water, mounding, and distance. Too many architects conceived of obstacles as a means to punish errant shots, whereas their original purpose was to render the game interesting. But championship golf was not alone responsible for the growing pains of golf architecture. A higher standard of living and the development of leisure activities were instrumental, while modern technological advances in irrigation and agronomy allowed golf courses to be maintained in excellent condition all year long, even in places where previously grass wouldn't naturally grow, such as the Arizona desert.

But how did golf course design evolve throughout the world? Old Scottish courses and modern American courses are so different that we cannot consider this due to mere chance. The two civilizations are manifested in the game of golf, which reflects each culture in small. The British are nurtured by a land inhabited for two thousand years, where a society slowly evolved. The Americans took possession of a land devoid of western culture until two centuries ago, and invented a new society. For the British, suffering builds character and happiness is not of this world, especially if one looks for it; it comes only after hardship, and then slowly. For Americans, happiness is on this Earth, especially American earth, developed thanks to American technology. Happiness must be an immediate reward; urgency is the American ethic. Yet America was peopled with Scottish immigrants who instilled in Americans the love of golf.

Yet the spread of golf beyond the Scottish moors—beginning in 1850—was brought about not only by a change in mentality or in nature, but by the 1848 invention of a more resistant ball, the gutta-percha. Golf architecture, our focus here, was brought about in turn by the absence of Scottish links in new golf territories. The respect for and imitation of nature are, in fact, the greatest illusions in golf architecture. This nature is tamed, ordered, forbidden to change or develop. It has become uniform, in the military sense of the word; colors, ranks, and cuts may change, but function is evident at first glance. Nature was simply arranged before, sometimes in the simplest way in the world—a case in point is the famous eighth hole at Troon, a par 3 nicknamed the "postage stamp" that was conceived merely by shaping a small dune for the tee and, 126 yards away, packing down a meadow where the sheep crossed. In the middle natural sand holes were left alone and served as defensive bunkers. Now nature had to be forced. It had to be manhandled, cut back, and reconstituted along the lines that the Creator had already established elsewhere. The links, which had been the ultimate golf course, became merely an original example, the degree zero or framework of the golf terrain, which could now depart from this point of reference.

In this century architects began to break apart the natural landscape, molding the earth into "strategic" or "penalizing" zones. The strategic hole aims to modulate risks and consequences: the better the shot, the easier, or at least more straightforward, the next one. The greater the error, the greater the resulting challenge. The penalizing hole, on the other hand, leaves no options; it's double or nothing. In this class we find island greens, fairways blocked by successive bunkers, and out-of-bounds

areas within the limits of the golf course.

Thus the landscape is definitely not incidental to the course—it is itself the essence of golf. The golf landscape is what we call, rather vulgarly, the "look" of a course; but perhaps a musical metaphor is more apt. The art of the course is like that of the harmony of sound. The lawns are the notes, the bunkers are the sharps, the water traps are the flats, the rough, the accidentals. The musical key is presented at the tee, the musical pause is found at the green. The final harmony is written on the scorecard.

THE LINKS

The links course is at once moor and *champ d'amour*. It is the naked earth, unadorned, absolutely natural. Great lovers always prefer the conquest of a beautiful woman without finery to that of an artificial creature. This rawness explains the hold that the links has on the golfer, although here, quite frankly, it is impossible to play golf for amusement. Short of the links, there is nothing; from it emanate all others. A links course architect arranges nature a bit, here and there, where God seemingly didn't have the time to tidy up the odds and ends. The architect can allow himself no further meddling, and here lies the danger: should he overshoot the mark he can never start again.

In Scotland strips of land stretch out, narrowly meandering between the sands bordering the sea and the first farmlands. They form a link between shore and inland; hence the name *links*. Nothing can be done with this land; even the stubborn sheep will not come to graze in the damp blades of grass bent by the wind. No, only golfers could find happiness here, for they are of another world, and the links is a moon where gusts of wind blow. Is it surprising, after all, that the only sport that has been played on the moon is golf? All of the golf courses that dot the Earth, in one way or another, measure themselves against the first links; even golf courses far from the sea pay it eternal homage. The links, in short, invented the scale of the golf landscape.

For the oldest of the links, the architect's name will remain forever anonymous. Before the end of the nineteenth century, given that nearly all golf courses that existed prior to 1850 were links, golf course architecture did not exist as such. No tees, no fairways, no greens. Nothing but lifeless surfaces, with commonly acknowledged points of departure and arrival, the fairways being the shortest route between them—though not necessarily the most direct. From its inception, the game entailed navigating as well as possible between the bunkers, the natural rough and the undulating land. Not until the very end of the nineteenth century were principles of golf architecture—reasoned, and not just imposed by nature—recorded.

Naturally, the art thus discovered was the domain of Scottish professional players, not amateurs. Instruction, manufacture of playing equipment, paid performances, and ultimately the construction of courses were for a long time the exclusive privilege of those who played the game full-time and who earned their living by it. Old Tom Morris had already constructed the New Course at Saint Andrews (1894) and had done the first drawing of Muirfield (1891). Later on he did not dare to attribute to himself the design for the Lahinch course; he had merely

indicated, on a plan drawn up by assistants, where to place the tees and the greens, the natural topography having always been fashioned to welcome a links. Another member of the same family, George Morris, would sign the first nine holes of the Hoylake course where the Frenchman Arnaud Massey won the British Open in 1907. A Dunn brother (Tom) conceived Wimbledon, one of the first courses to be built outside Scotland. But the first "intellectual" reference for golf architecture is due a historic winner of the British Open, Willie Park, in his 1896 *The*

Game of Golf. Most of his advice, of course, referred to the links. What would it teach future generations? Only respect and prudence—perhaps even timidity—faced with the natural terrain.

The pioneers of the sport barely dared even to indicate boundaries—and it certainly wasn't because the shepherd's lobby opposed it. Golfers played golf—or gouff, gowf, or cofl, as it was still called—where they could, without choosing a terrain and without modifying it. The Old Course at Saint Andrews once had twenty-two holes, until it was cut back to eighteen as the great city of the time, capital of the kingdom of Scotland, claimed part of the grounds to build houses on. Perth had only seven holes, Prestwick only twelve until 1883—even though the British Open had been played there as early as 1860. True, these ancestors of the modern course had no points of reference. To what could they compare themselves when nothing else had been invented? Those who were called upon a little later to participate in the expansion of golf—prompted by the invention of the gutta-percha ball, an event that wreaked havoc—would fall unconsciously into the trap of attempting to re-create a links course on the inland. The blind hole or shot so characteristic in the undulating links, for example, found itself denatured in the valley inland course through a fear of disturbing a virgin landscape sadly less fit for golf than Scotland's seaside. The inland valley's slight undulations, as if the earth had not been entirely smoothed out, can be sensed under the feet and in the rolling of the ball, but can barely be seen with the naked

eye. The real, if subtle, reliefs of this flat country guide the ball into its tufts of grass, if one knows how to read them. Rolling golf reigns here.

But the links has a second relief that cannot be seen, though it is sometimes heard and always inhaled: the wind. As the ball glides through it, it must hold its own. The wind envelops it, skirts around it, helps or hinders it in its path. The wind that embraces the landscape of the links sculpts the game, even if it seems to leave the ground untouched; only the high grasses creak and bend when the North Wind or a mild sea breeze blows.

Rather than proudly controlling the ball, the golfer must learn to strike a deal with the wind. The challenge of the links course is above all found in an understanding of the wind, and that is what separates the stroller from the golfer.

SAINT ANDREWS

No one knows who built it. (The first recognized designer is Allan Robertson, who became the pro and clubmaker of Saint Andrews. He is credited with widening the Old Course and creating the seventeenth green.) In spite, or perhaps because, of this the Old Course at Saint Andrews has served as an inspiration for dozens of successive generations of architects. It is the ultimate links, a bare landscape upon which it would be impossible to imagine anything other than magic lawn, an immense strip of straight fairway.

Like most good links courses the terrain of Saint Andrews is a perpetually undulating carpet, from the tee to the green. Rarely does the player benefit from a level stance or a level lie. He must continually adapt himself to a golfer's relief that appears flat to anyone else. In some ways, however, the architecture of the links seems passé; it does not require a long carry from the tee, for instance, and is filled with numerous blind bunkers. It is often said that some mornings new, previously unknown bunkers are discovered, perhaps born of a gust of wind during the night ... The stuff of legends, no doubt; but the Old Course is indeed legendary. Not everything was invented here, but here a model was fixed for an ever-evolving posterity that continually refers back to its source as it progresses.

The challenge of its authenticity begins at the first hole with the Swilcan Burn, a little stream that cuts right in front of the green. It is the ideal water hazard, just wide enough to impede the golfer in the last yards of the ball's flight without coming too soon. It requires the golfer to make a perfect second shot, the supreme test of nerve and skill.

And the adventure continues, practically in a straight line since all the holes follow one another along the Scottish Sea—the Firth of Firth and Saint Andrews Bay—until the course turns around and makes its way back to the clubhouse, parallel to the holes going out, often sharing their greens. The howling wind is a constant companion. Bunkers riddle the terrain. These bunkers are no doubt natural depressions, dug by sheep trying to protect themselves from the wind.

A golf course in Scotland can change every fifteen minutes. On the fourteenth hole of Saint Andrews, the golfer must avoid going out of bounds and the lineup of "Beardies Bunkers." An esplanade is christened, ironically, the Champs Elysées: this 564-yard-long par 5 isn't very wide. Next the golfer has to pass over the Ginger Beer bunker and the prophetically named Grave. Will he

succeed? It's up to the wind. For the wind is not the same on the ground as in the air where, in an instant, the ball will fly, and may even change directions in the interim. Of course the golfer can play it safe, to the right or to the left, as the hole is not penalizing, but strategic. This will simply require a third stroke with displaced feet. And the road toward the Valley of Sin is still long, where the final illusions are reaped before the last green.

The venerable caddies mutter at this point, "It need a heid to play gowf."

Designed "naturally" since the fifteenth century; official date 1754 (when the rules of the game were established). Old Course 6566 yards, par 72; New Course 6604 yards, par 71; Jubilee Course 6805 yards, par 72; Eden Course 6315 yards, par 70. All courses are located in the City of Saint Andrews.

BALLYBUNION

The wilderness can be tamed, perhaps. A lifetime would be needed to tame Ballybunion. In western Ireland, a land of ghosts, a golf course drunken with greenery has been carved from the surf and the rocks. One could say that it didn't dare to stretch itself over the moors, but preferred to curl up into the hollows of its linksland. It seems to be sound asleep.

Further west a breeze kicks up. It is the wind of County Kerry which comes and never leaves, for here is its home. Ballybunion is wild and will remain so. It is not possible to beat this course. You may surprise it, you may inexplicably get lucky; a very good player might dominate it here and there, but never subdue it. Ballybunion is a lion that sooner or later will devour its tamer.

All attempts have been made. The old seventeenth and eighteenth holes, two monstrous par 5s surpassing 500 yards, were reordered as the fourth and fifth holes— 504 and 508 yards respectively—due to the positioning of a new clubhouse. The holes are the same, but attacking them at this point in the game diminishes the tension of facing them at the end of the round. But still, the 6503 yards of this unearthly links must be covered in 71 strokes, and even when the wind mysteriously dies down, they have never been mastered in less than 67. Formidable Ballybunion is surely the golf course closest to the sea, nestled in the Shannon Estuary, studded with hills and dunes where the tall shining grasses sway back and forth in a continual, seductive, and dangerous dance.

Much later one of the most formidable creators, Robert Trent-Jones, was brought in to build a "New Course" on an adjacent moor. His attempts to equal the Old Course's severity were in vain; the New Course can-

not equal the savagery of Nature's work. The long, straight, sloping fairways of the Old—riddled with bunkers and hollows, ending with small greens in an arena of knolls that lie in wait for balls—cannot be duplicated. The race of wild golf courses can boast a few kings. Ballybunion is even more than this; it is an emperor in the land of the Celts.

Designed at the end of the nineteenth century on the shores of the Shannon Estuary. Established in 1896. New course by Robert Trent-Jones, designed after World War II, 6479 yards, par 72. Old Course 6503 yards, par 71. Approximately one-half mile south of Ballybunion, County Kerry.

TRALEE/WATERVILLE

Nothing happens overnight in the world of golf. There was a long wait before Arnold Palmer brought his expert eye and architectural talents to Europe for the first time, long after he had eagled his first holes on the greens of the Old World in the early 1960s.

But sometimes the golf course permits immediate success stories. A case in point is the Tralee course, unanimously recognized as one of the most authentic of links courses recently constructed. It should be noted that few such courses are built, as if the enthusiasm of golf course architects was dampened by existing natural wonders. Arnold Palmer, king of the game and king of the lawn, finally dared, and succeeded. Today on the southwest coast of County Kerry lies a golf course that seems to be a gift from God, there from the beginning of time. Yet it is one of the newest golf courses in the world, having opened in 1986. Its only departure from the original rigid architecture of the links is the use of wide bunkers a little less deep than those made naturally by the wind. But the entire layout of the links is lovingly repeated here, with its long fairways undulating between the dunes, the high grasses bent but never bro-

ken by the wind, the sandy soil, and an uninterrupted view all the way to the first Brandon mountains.

The same pastoral scene, a symphony of lakes and of the Atlantic, is played out just a few miles from Tralee at the famous golf course of Waterville, so aptly named. The course is surrounded on three sides by the ocean. The wind blows straight; here it is the golfer that swirls around. Confronted with some of the narrowest fairways in the world—curving to follow the contours of the coast and immediately bordered by high and dense rough—and an enormous distance, approaching 7300 yards—nearly a world record—the player is sometimes in a hurry just to return to the sumptuous hotel that dominates the entrance to the course.

Still, humor has its place here. Local tradition assigns names to the holes; that called Broadway actually evokes the well-deserved reward of the player capable, so they say, of shooting a birdie on this eighteenth hole. During the World Cup played at Waterville in 1978, the sport's champions acknowledged its astonishing succession of turning-point holes—holes at which the entire structure of the game can turn upside-down because of a gust of wind or a choice of strategy. Sam Snead has dubbed Waterville the "Magnificent Monster."

Tralee: designed by Arnold Palmer along the west coast of County Kerry. Course created in 1986. 6613 yards, par 71. Approximately 8 miles from Tralee.

Waterville: designed by Eddie Hackett and John A. Mulcany on the shores of the Atlantic. Modified Course opened in 1970. 7238 yards, par 73. On eastern edge of the Bay of Ballingskelligs.

ROYAL JERSEY/ LA MOYE

Are we in France or Great Britain? Neither. The island of Jersey may partake of both cultures, but it is self-sufficient. For a Frenchman, the vagabond specter of Victor Hugo haunts the landscape. For the golfer, the reality of Jersey's golf courses may be enough.

One is public, the other private; but it is not merely words or symbols that differentiate them. The public course, the Royal Jersey Golf Club, extends along a moor bordered on one side by the sea and on the other by the city. As in times past, it is open to all, even non-golfers. Anyone may stroll through it; after all, it is the path—the *link*, in its original sense—from the farmland to the sea.

The island's second golf course, the La Moye Club, is private. Despite the change of ambiance, this course is as authentic as the first. This time, the venerable club members welcome you on the steps of the clubhouse; you must give your qualifications and experience, and know—intuitively or through previous apprenticeship—the etiquette and customs. In the evening, as the sun sets on the far side of the dunes which shelter the greens, beer and warm whiskey flow liberally, along with traditional tales, late into the night. Meanwhile the distant flags—raised high above the dunes to signal holes hidden on the greens in deep basins—flutter in the wind.

Royal Jersey: designed by an unknown architect in 1878. 6030 yards, par 70. Four miles from Saint Helier.

La Moye: designed by Georges Boomer in 1902. 6464 yards, par 72. Five miles from Saint Helier.

ROYAL SAINT GEORGE'S

If you chance to fall asleep on the flight to Sandwich, you may awake suddenly and think yourself in Scotland. Facing the coast of France in southern England, this centuries-old, venerable links nestles along the coast near the tiny city of Sandwich, with its narrow streets designed by the Romans long before fairways were built.

A bourgeois colony came down from London to this "gray Côte d'Azur" on the south of the isle at the end of the nineteenth century and established the first club. A doctor and golfer, Laidlaw Purves, drew the first course, as the story goes, by "climbing to the top of the tower of Sandwich and observing the landscape with a golfer's eye." The result was an incredibly authentic links course, faithful to its Scottish models and respectful of the nature of the site. Many years later, in about 1975, Frank Pennink substantially modified the original design to eliminate anachronisms for the modern game: too many blind shots (on the par 3s for instance), holes that were too short, and bunkers that needed rearrangement. But the fundamental character of the course's layout was retained. In fact, a few years ago (in 1985) the British Open—which is always played on a links, even outside of Scotland—rediscovered this passionate course in its tranquil setting.

For the Royal Saint George's has a links layout—indeed, in the strictest sense of the term; it has evolved through the decades of golf played on it. A large bunker in the center of the fourth fairway, about 200 yards from the tee, was never designed and never chosen—a small depression here grew "naturally" in the right location, dug by the successive balls played there. Neither the architect nor Nature is in control of the course's design; the game creates itself.

The designers of the Royal Saint George's aimed to put together an ideal synthesis of the links. What is demanded of a great first hole? To be free of obstructions—it is as concrete as that—but more, to whet the player's appetite, letting him test some of the parameters that the course will offer later on. Thus, the first hole at the Royal Saint George's requires a classic drive, yet by the second shot the golfer must already shift stances, as so often on a links course. In front of the green, a row of bunkers appears, protecting a sloping surface behind it. In the same way, the first nine holes build a score and the following nine put to the test the skills acquired— often a losing proposition.

Championships, British Opens, and amateur competitions have all been played at Royal Saint George's. And even literature has had its day—the famous match between James Bond and Goldfinger in Ian Fleming's novel is played here, although the course was renamed the Royal Saint-Marks for the occasion.

Designed in the south of England in 1897 by Dr. Laidlaw Purves on the dunes, and modified in 1975 by Frank Pennink. 6860 yards, par 70. A few miles from the city of Sandwich.

MUIRFIELD

The links created golf course architecture without knowing it. Muirfield, where the Honourable Company of Golfers of Edinburgh has had its headquarters since the end of the nineteenth century, is a case in point, having blended together contradictory concepts from its founding.

Long before the establishment of two opposed schools of golf architecture, the "penalizing" and the "strategic"—generally attributed to the appearance of inland courses—some of the old links already had a dual aspect. The eighth hole at Muirfield, with its cascading bunkers on the right and its dogleg on the left, forcefully dictates the route to take; to deviate could be

costly. After Walter Hagen succeeded in finding a new right-hand route in the 1929 British Open, trees were planted in 1930 to reinstate the forced trajectory. The penalizing hole had been invented, long before it became the rage in the United States in the 1930s.

The 515-yard, par 5, ninth hole, on the other hand, is a famous example of the opposite strategy. A very long drive is obviously needed to reach the green in two shots. This is possible only if the wind isn't against you, but even if it's with you the drive must be powerful just so the second shot will not be too taxing. The fairway seems to shrink, crunched between the rough on both sides and two bunkers on the left. The second shot must be per-

fectly placed and strong at the same time, two essentials that are often mutually exclusive. An out-of-bounds marked by a wall of ancient gray stones borders the left side of the hole. This is a heroic hole *par excellence*.

So many basic golf course concepts were established at this club! It originally extended to Musselburg, although here we are only examining its current design; the first rules of the game were written here in 1744, ten years before Saint Andrews. The current Muirfield is also one of the first courses where the principle of an "out" nine and an "in" nine was accepted. This allows for an infinite variety in the sequence of pars; only once does

the player have three consecutive holes with the same alignment. Thus he is forced to try out the wind from all directions, without getting used to it.

Muirfield is a school in itself not only because of its design, but because of its soul. One of the oldest golf clubs in the world, it maintains a tradition and discipline that every visitor—few are accepted as members—respects, as if in a grass-lined cathedral.

Designed by Old Tom Morris on the moor outside of Edinburgh. Club established in 1744, current course built in 1891. 6946 yards, par 72. Approximately 13 miles from Berwick, and about 48 miles from Edinburgh.

LE TOUQUET

A re-creation that is not recreational: thus could be defined the golf course of Le Touquet, the most links-like course in France.

A re-creation, because Le Touquet was one of the most heavily damaged regions in France after World War II, given its location in the north of the country. As has been done elsewhere, another course could have been created in its place. Nothing remained of the former course but the blueprints and the determination of those who loved this terrain, who in more carefree times had passed some of their finest holidays on this Anglo-French coast. With plans in hand the great course was literally unearthed, almost in its entirety. Ten years were required to trace the original layout and to return the course to health. But the result was superb—certainly no mere diversion, even if the player's pleasure on this rare French links is absolute. The player must humbly perfect his game, and the course will respond.

We often hear of *La Mer,* the Sea Course, which is a truly spectacular links, but Le Touquet also boasts the Forest Course, *La Forêt.* Adjacent to the Sea Course, it is older, a little shorter, and slightly less defined, but immensely interesting. The Sea Course is grandiose. Its first holes are tranquil; lying slightly inland, where they link up with the final holes, they come to seem like a haven. For in the middle are fairy-tale dunes whose colors change as the clouds pass overhead and in which are hidden numerous bunkers, blind spots, and small greens.

It is as if Scotland had been reconstituted in France:

the steadily-blowing wind at Le Touquet determines one's strategy, as on any true links. The course more than once straddles the crest of a dune, guiding the player through tough ravines full of bushes rustling from the last balls that took refuge in them. The 6715-yard course starts off deceptively with three par 5s interrupted by a more modest par 4, and offers the player the challenge of many strokes that can change from day to day, even from one quarter-hour to the next. Le Touquet is an inventive, audacious course.

Designed on the dunes by W. Ferrie and J. Taylor. Sea Course opened 1939, 6715 yards, par 72. Forest Course opened 1903, 6463 yards, par 71. Rebuilt after the war by C. Lafontan, opening again in 1958. Three miles from the city of Le Touquet.

THE INLAND PLAIN COURSE

Eternal land, with its forests, its meadows of hardy vegetation where wild animals can always find sustenance, rich and self-sufficient ... Suddenly man arrives, imposing silence and re-inventing the landscape, trimming the forest and planting lawns in the meadows, chasing away the animals and inviting in their place other men to play golf. Thus, the inland course is born.

The links is the purest example of the discovered—not invented—golf course. On the links it was merely a question of finishing the work left in fallow by an undesignated Creator. The inland courses, however, marked the discovery of golf course architecture, adding a dimension of vanity. Here it was no longer a question of completing what had been left undone, but of "playing God"—creating something new from the land. Nature would now follow man's orders, not force man to obey her whims.

It was only at the end of the nineteenth century that inland courses first met with success, when the discovery of terrains to the west of London—which offered the unique character of being both flat and atop a sandy soil—met with great enthusiasm. Courses far from the sea had already been built, but on non-porous clay soil. This time around it seemed as if the impossible had been accomplished. There was no doubt an element of chance involved in the design: these new courses were laid out in concentric circles while the older ones adopted the straight lines dictated by natural topography. In any case, the older ones were not really designed but rather adapted from the existing conditions. This time it was necessary to plan before cutting into nature. The land chosen by the first men that took it upon themselves to thus re-create nature was not only untouched, but was not at all suited to the game. The idea that man could break through the forest to draw fairways required a true

cultural upheaval. It had never even been imagined before, much less attempted. It was only golf's inner drive to seek new territory that could push its architects to this point. After all, golf could have been considered a game only possible on bare moors, a seaside art, as in fact it had been defined until then. It was as if man had decided to ski without mountains or to play tennis on sloping courts.

This revolutionary expansion also allowed the game to break out of its narrow framework—literally narrow, since the links was by definition only a strip of land between the sand and the first tillable soil. With the inland course this corridor was shattered. The "return to the clubhouse" after the ninth hole was an outgrowth of inland course design, primarily because in a plain the land is structured in squares rather than elongated strips. Financing, too, was often lacking to construct a full eighteen holes immediately. On the scorecard "in" and "out" still referred to the two halves of the course; but by the time a party had gotten "out" they were already back "in." It was almost as if these pioneer inland architects were afraid of blasphemizing the links—their only reference, the true mother golf—or at least of being weaned from it too soon.

The inland established strong points of reference for ensuing courses, however; today many features introduced with the inland course seem completely natural. Many of these were possibly due to the benefit of reconstructing Nature in its entirety rather than adapting to it, but this should not lessen the impact of those who dared to break the Scottish mold and turn things upside-down. The two competing schools of the "penalizing" and the "strategic" hole are indelibly linked to the artistic freedom that the inland allowed, even imposed. The penalizing hole allows the player only one plan of attack; if very difficult it becomes "heroic"—although the current theories of Robert Trent-Jones consider this as a third class, it is really a sub-category of the first. If the player does not master this single approach, the hole penalizes the errant shot without offering an alternative. This is the

"make or break" that players refer to, somewhat superstitiously, at the start of a game. This is also the origin of the "double or nothing" holes with their island greens that we find in modern American architecture. A century later, the inland is still exploring its most fantasmagoric nooks and crannies.

The strategic hole, on the other hand, gives the player at least two options, one generally—though not always—easier than the other. The principle of the strategic hole lies not in this hierarchy of risk, however, but rather in the adaptation to it, the style of the second stroke and the final score that results from the chosen strategy. The strategic hole, to be sure, penalizes the player who does not master it, but it offers a choice.

KILLARNEY

Golf was played at Killarney well before the turn of the century. A course dating from 1891 spread out across land rented from the Earl of Kenmare for the symbolic sum of one guinea. In 1936 the rent was raised to seventy-five guineas, and outraged club members asked the Earl if they could instead use another terrain, useless for farming, on the sandy shores of the neighboring lakes. Permission was granted. After three years of work following the plans of Sir Guy Campbell the new course was opened on October 3, 1939—practically unnoticed in the shadow of World War II.

At the same time Lord Castlerosse—a legendary figure of British high society, a scratch player, and an ardent enthusiast of golf course architecture—succeeded his father as Earl of Kenmare. He brought in a celebrated golf observer, Henry Longhurst, and the two set about redesigning the old golf course, considerably modifying eight holes and building five new ones. The two men had conceived an instant success, a golf marvel watched over by the Kerry mountains, with their purple evening hues reflected in the lakes of Lough Lean.

In the 1970s demands from visitors and champions intensified and another parcel of Kenmare land was prepared for the construction of a second eighteen-hole course, the Mahony's Point Course, next to Killeen's. Taken separately, each course is of the highest technical level; combined for the championships, they constitute one of the most extraordinary and surprising natural inland courses on the planet.

The composite championship course begins calmly enough but ends its first half in a flurry of three par 4s measuring respectively 402, 423, and 449 yards, a total of over 1300 yards to polish off in no more than twelve strokes. The same progression is found on the way in: two consecutive par 5s, then a third, the sixteenth hole measuring 518 yards, the longest hole on the course, followed by a par 4 of over 400 yards and finally a par 3 on the last hole, a rarity. This is one of the purest short holes in the world—nevertheless measuring 202 yards. Henry Longhurst described this hole, flanked by a green protected on the right by a curtain of trees and on the left by a straight bunker, as "a lovely place to die." It is rivaled only by the infamous thirteenth hole, a par 5 of 480 yards. This seemingly modest hole requires a remarkable drive to keep the ball on the green—bordered by bunkers, trees, and even a road—on the second shot. In total, the par 73 composite course measures a monumental 6758 yards with at least twelve holes protected by trees yet bordering the sea and lakes. It is home to several important championships; here Gary Player first participated in a tournament outside South Africa. He did not win, but later admitted that some of its holes were among the purest "inlands" on the five continents.

Designed by Sir Guy Campbell, Lord Castlerosse, and Henry Longhurst. Killeen: opened in 1939, 6987 yards, par 73. Mahoney's Point: opened in 1972, 6728 yards, par 72. Composite course 6758 yards, par 73. Located in southwestern Ireland, equidistant from Cork and Shannon.

SUNNINGDALE/ WENTWORTH

After a first visit to Sunningdale the great Bobby Jones said, "I would like to take it home with me in my luggage." Home for him was already Augusta. No doubt about it, Wentworth and Sunningdale are both part of the same prestigious family of dream inland courses.

Wentworth, located near Windsor Castle, is dominated by a Victorian clubhouse. Slightly further down the eighteen holes are nestled in age-old pines and shrubs pastel-hued in places, bright yellow and violet in others. From the start the player finds himself in the midst of long carries to the green which must be skillfully aimed down fairways framed by omnipresent trees. Arnold Palmer has described the seventeenth hole as one of the most beautiful long holes in the world. And that is precisely what the great architect H. S. Colt, an avid proponent of the inland course, aimed for when he designed it. The East Course was completed in 1924 and the West Course—today home to the Wentworth championship—in 1926, at Virginia Waters near London.

Sunningdale is both a historical landmark and a champions' meeting point, top-level competitions having consistently been played here. Just as Saint Andrews is the ultimate links, Sunningdale is the perfect inland course. The champion pioneer Willie Park, who sketched the Old Course's design in 1900, is considered the father of inland architecture in the early twentieth century. (A second course at Sunningdale was designed in 1922 by

H. S. Colt, the creator of Wentworth.) At Sunningdale, everything conspires to push the player toward a strategic game. After an apparently wide-open tee-off, the holes seem to solidify and suddenly all of their hidden challenges appear: bunkers, narrowings, trees leaning dangerously close to the center of the fairway, and shadowy greens which seem to sleep and await only a three-ball match. Half of these greens are on promontories, plateaus atop hills that roll all too gently; this great course demands skill in the art of chipping.

Sunningdale: Old Course designed in 1900 by Willie Park, 6586 yards, par 72. New Course designed in 1922 by H. S. Colt, 6565 yards, par 70. Twenty-five miles from London. Wentworth: designed in 1920 by H. S. Colt, 6945 yards, par 72. Twenty miles from London.

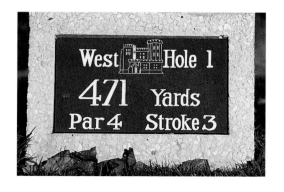

LES BORDES

Of all the courses in this book, Les Bordes is the newest, opened in 1987. Indeed, when one considers the Scottish dictum "Seed and mow. For 200 years," it is practically a newborn lawn. If time and survival are justifiably prized in a golf course, still we must admit that Les Bordes International Golf Course is a prodigy, fit to stand among the great veterans.

At the request of Baron Bich, who had become a devoted admirer of the old and noble game, and in association with Sakurai of Japan, the American architect Robert Van Hagge designed this showcase for the beauties of golf in the countryside of Sologne. Les Bordes is clearly an inland course, deep in the interior of France, far from sea air and alongside one of the most beautiful forests in the country. But within these parameters Robert Van Hagge combined concepts from a broad spectrum of golf architecture, boldly mixing traditions of different countries, continents, and periods. How did he do it?

Some holes are constructed like those of the Scottish links, with their rolling hills and slanted knolls; others are purely Californian with water hazards extending the length of the fairway; others have island greens, calling for a double-or-nothing approach (which is, with the bunkers of grass that one finds here and there at Les Bordes, one of the characteristics of ultra-modern late-twentieth-century golf architecture). Finally, some have classic doglegs, propped against the twelve holes with water hazards at which one encounters all types of bunkers: flat and long, dug out and buried, with thick or thin rims.

This course might seem like a trial lesson, presenting a catalog of styles and lacking in unity, were its force not so overwhelming. Instead it is a fabulous gem, merciless in its fluctuating brilliance, set in the heart of the French countryside.

Designed in 1987 by Robert Van Hagge. 7012 yards, par 72. Forty miles from Orléans.

CHANTILLY

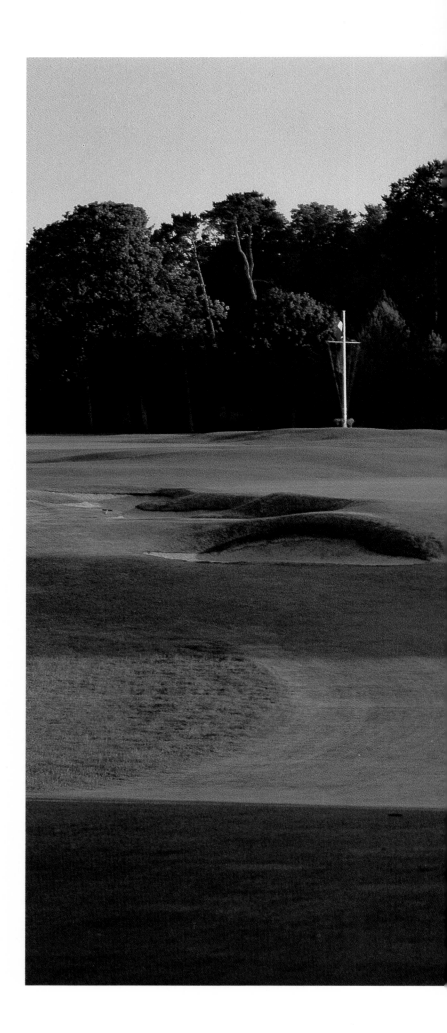

The principal obstacle at Chantilly is anxiety. This majestic course has been so talked-about—though never discredited—that all those who tackle it, even its members, often carry extra balls with them in their bags before teeing off from the first hole—a justifiable precaution.

More than many other landscapes, the course at Chantilly is a theater of green. From the terrace of the clubhouse an unforgettable view unfolds, ample and undulating, almost evoking the rolling hills of a links. Yet the golfer soon discovers the most typical of inland courses. The holes spread in several directions like a starburst, a great symphony of lawn. Chantilly means to assert its place in the highest and most ancient golf tradition (it has been called the Continental annex of Saint Andrews), however, and the hole furthest from the clubhouse is the ninth, at the other end of the forest.

This forest, though it never closes in completely, cannot be bypassed. Here and there bare plateaus offer light on a long rigorous road, on which shot after shot confirms that the master, early-twentieth-century architect Tom Simpson left nothing to chance. In the best of circumstances the golfer needs all his skill to communicate with this noble course. If the wind blows or if the Scottish-style rough has grown knee-deep, nothing short of perfection will do. The placing of a shot is never

simple and never allows for an easy second shot, but a poorly chosen strategy allows no way out. There are two secrets at Chantilly. The drive has to reach a good third down the fairway—the only way to ensure a second shot of human proportions—and the lines must be accurately read and judged. In simple language, the putt should be made inside of a typical line. Only old veterans of the course have fought long enough to understand that Chantilly demands not only a perfect game, but even more challenging, a noble one too.

Designed in 1908 by Tom Simpson; opened in September of 1909. 7215 yards, par 71. About 20 miles from Paris.

BREMEN ZUR VAHR

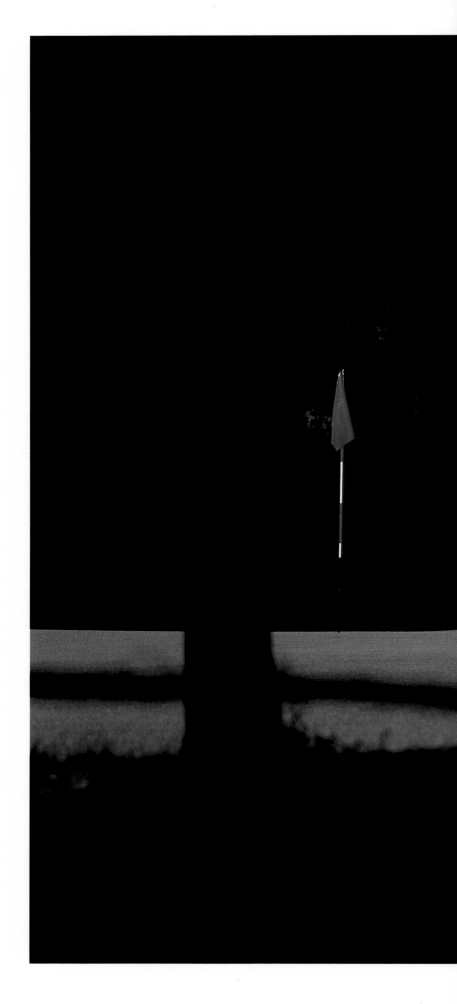

This course employs a powerful architecture: heavy, Germanic, imposing. The flat course of Bremen Zur Vahr plunges into the German forest for an interminable distance, its flatness attractively enhanced by the relief of rows of trees, shrubbery, and evening shadows. A colossus among lawns, it easily surpasses 7200 yards from the back tees. Fortunately for the scorecard, an unusual number of par 5s—six in total—make the course a par 74. All this is unusual on paper, but the terrain presents a respectable classicism.

Although its present inland course was designed relatively recently, Bremen's roots go further back. A distinction must be made here between the club and the course itself. The club, founded at the beginning of the twentieth century, offers its members of the German *haute bourgeoisie* traditional social activities like tennis and bridge as well as golf. The course has been modified a number of times, most recently in 1962. There was no need to seek out a star architect: the club's former president and a local technician designed these marvelous forest fairways. It's difficult to err when one knows the course and its setting intimately, from longstanding practice.

Despite its numerous par 5s, reaching or surpassing at times 574 yards from the back tees (fortunately amateurs and ladies can take advantage of tees that are at times advanced substantially), Bremen Zur Vahr is also a paradise for long and difficult par 4s, not uncommon on very long courses. Here the golfer must utilize all his tal-

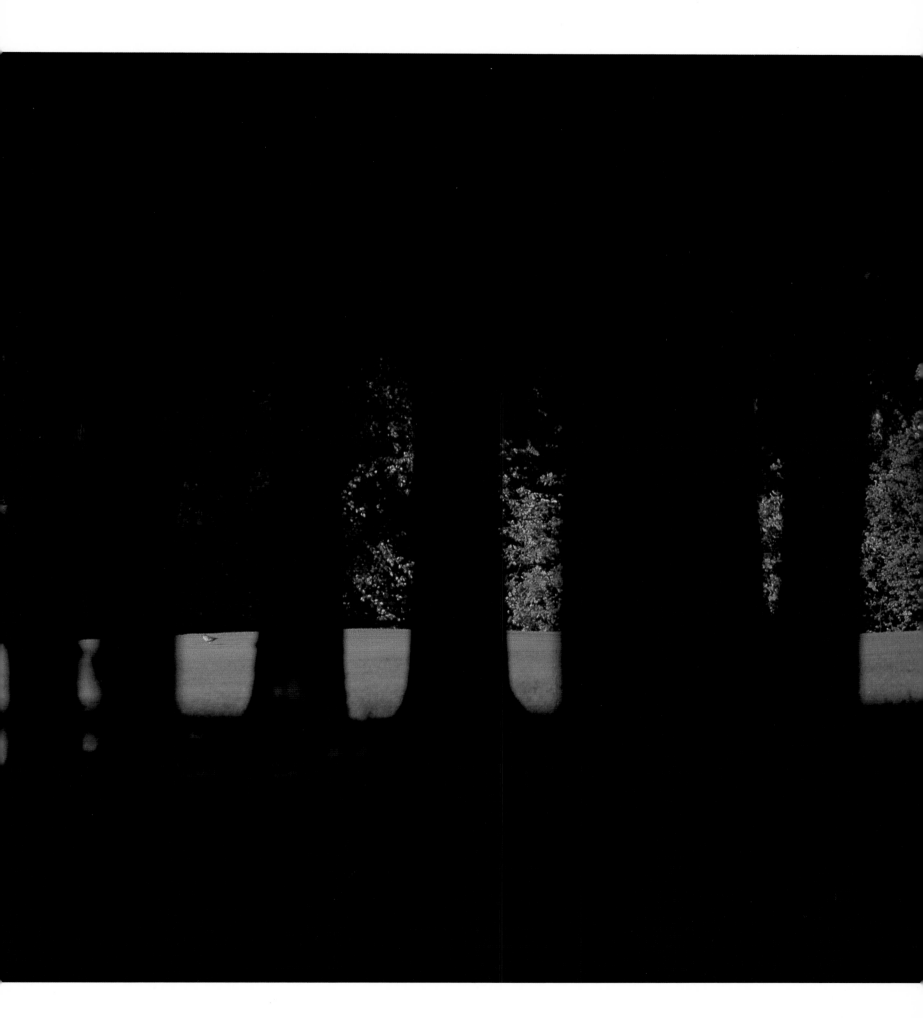

ents with no margin for error, since a powerful second shot must land on the green. Aside from some recent creations, there are very few bunkers: twenty-four in all. Their rims are a little lean, as if fixed in an ironic grin, waiting for the balls to arrive. Here and there in the crook of a dogleg are little wooden huts shaded by the trees, where one imagines restful encounters. At the end of the long road is the clubhouse, its dark roof sheltering a terrace at the foot of which the scores are tallied. It is a haven of peace after the long walk, a club where staunch tradition and ultimate sport have always mingled in perfect harmony.

Designed by Bernhard von Limburger and Auguste Weyhausen. Club established in 1905. Course modified in the 1960s. 7262 yards, par 74. Eight miles from Bremen.

RAVENSTEIN

Ravenstein is deceptive. At first glance, it is a great course among other great courses. Yet it isn't exactly like the others.

Its official name, "The Royal Belgian Golf Club," is not contrived. At the beginning of the twentieth century, King Leopold II made the royal domain of Ravenstein in the commune of Tervueren available to the sport's earliest enthusiasts. (The king of Belgium remains the club's honorary president and all of its activities are linked to the royal family.) Complete with its chateau and splendid park, it awaited only the arrival of an architect whose creations are still admired today, the Englishman Tom Simpson. Seated solidly on its throne before the putting green, the chateau with its outlying buildings is the model of an architecturally balanced clubhouse, reposing sturdily on its foundations. One could say that Ravenstein has a solid stance.

The course is also deceptive in its development. Ravenstein's par 73 (whose length from the back tees surpasses 6600 yards) is composed not of a greater number of par 5s, but rather of a reduced number of par 3s. Consequently the many par 4s do not demand powerful drives but the diabolical precision so typical of courses designed by Simpson. A typically inland landscape, the course imposes variety: the first seven holes, for example, never offer two of the same pars in a row, following which the player has to tackle five consecutive par 4s from the seventh through the eleventh holes. Simpson's greens are targets to be tackled from the open

side, assuming the first shot is placed well, or else over obstacles (there are no water hazards here, only bunkers). Often the bunkers push their sides ahead toward the green, their edges swelling to form a mound which can be deceptive from a distance. The architecture is typically strategic, establishing a scale of penalties rather than an "all or nothing" approach. The white fences—not to be confused with the wickets of the same color that indicate the rare out-of-bounds of this royal do-main—impart, more than anything else, a feeling of security. This vast enclosure's enormous acreage enables the course to burst forth amid thick rows of dark trees and a counterpoint of mauve flowers, ensuring absolute isolation to the golfer in search of self.

Designed by Tom Simpson at the beginning of the twentieth century on the domain made available by the royal family of Belgium. Opened in 1906. 6651 yards, par 73. Six miles from Brussels.

THE INLAND VALLEY COURSE

A golf course is never flat. However, the "golfer's relief," the slope that will often influence the game, is rarely visible to the naked eye. It is scarcely perceptible on the greens, and from a distance, seems inconsistent on the fairways. The slope of a valley may be visible, but usually it is not the one in play.

And that is the trap. The flat areas of a landscape

are only illusions which, with the even more perilous illusion of distance, are most frequently responsible for a player's poor score. Indeed, we forget that golf is only a game of reactions. We may understand courses instinctively, as do gifted players, or empirically—by dissecting the laws of ballistics—as do the self-taught or the old breed of caddies. The result is always the same. The struggle between the practice and the theory of golf begins as soon as one must swing on an incline. A system of compensatory laws aims to help the ball remain on target in spite of everything: if the ball is lower than one's feet it will tend to take to the air as a slice. If it is positioned downhill it will have to be hit with a healthy dose of top spin. But a perfectly straight departure on a perfectly flat terrain, and following a perfectly vertical swing—which arithmetic tells us will have a margin of error of zero—does not exist, as it implies swinging the head of the club through one's own feet.

The advent of the inland valley course only compli-

cated things further. The small valley is not a golf topography, though it is a pleasure to view. Too ample to provide anything but a pleasant setting, it serves to enhance the decor rather than to modify the game. Thus the small valley can almost be considered an obstacle—not as described in the rule book, but rather from a strategic perspective. The true role of an obstacle, at least as it is defined in golf, is not to penalize a bad shot, but to make the game more interesting! Since the small valley is itself an obstacle, the inland valley course will always be an imperfect landscape. This is rarely intentional; more than anywhere else, these imposing earthy masses would frighten any designer. Nature is here in the rough, with its great hills and its grassy, tree-covered slopes. It is seductive, at times beautiful. Yet we never weary of the sleight-of-hand with which the valley's slopes distract attention from the true cause of the ball's deviation from its course: the more subtle contours which we can barely discern. We never cease to marvel at this semi-mountain that practically prohibits the game from being played. It's hypnotic! The landscape seems alive with rolling hills, as if giant swells of grass made the game list from side to side.

The inland valley even has its own byproducts, blind shots and blind holes. A blind shot may confront the player unable to follow the main line toward the hole; this curt rebuke from the course is legitimate when the conversation has turned ugly due to the golfer's error. But what can be said of a course that imposes a penalty by nature of its very structure? This is a true defect—the golf course must be honest. The inland valley sometimes offers a sinister retort to a player whose commitment is entirely honorable. For example, a straight, strong drive, landing exactly where it should, may be followed by a blind shot. One might say that this blindness is absolute

only the first time; once played, the hole is no longer blind. True, the effect is absolute only the first time, but the disturbance persists every time that follows. Little by little, of course, the player will learn to perfectly visualize the layout of a blind hole, but he will never be playing with true vision. On a flat inland the blind hole is a mistake, since everything is "planned." Worse still are the flags that are only half visible, the semi-blinds. Where exactly is the hole: at the end of the green, in the middle, at the beginning?

There are, of course, blind holes on many links courses, but most of the time they are only "blind receptacles," greens on which small dunes hide the hole while still indicating its general whereabouts. Though the target may be hidden, its position is visible. The reverse is true of the genuine blind shot sometimes imposed by the inland valley. If there was an abyss after a plateau, in this case, it would be impossible to guess. The player can only imagine what is beyond, and this is not the way golf

should be played. The golf course should not play tricks. It is the golfer's role to be clever, to use creative powers infinitely superior to those of the course. The latter's advantage is in its strength. Fortunately the blind shot is merely an anomaly, a twist imposed by the inland valley landscape, just as the island green is an exaggeration of the "American" landscape.

Teeing off from a hilly inland the player begins a great adventure, pushing back the valley's horizon as he gracefully advances the ball. It is a landscape on which one of the ceaseless quests of the golfer is within reach from the first shot: isolation.

GLENEAGLES

There may still live a rare, blessed few who played golf with the famous triumvirate of the early twentieth century, Taylor, Vardon, and Braid—a small boy who stood in the shadow of these first sacred megaliths would today be in his nineties. Time marches on: but James Braid marked his passage with an indelible memorial when he sketched the first plan for the Gleneagles golf course in Scotland. The great champion, already advanced in years, put aside any inhibitions when he chose a setting in the center of the Highlands to build one of the rare inland courses in this land of links. Gleneagles is considered the peak of an architecture invented little by little during a turbulent era. The early construction of Gleneagles was interrupted by World War I; it began again once the war was over, and the first two courses were inaugurated before 1920. The majestic hotel that dominates this architectural ensemble was built several years later as Braid had wished.

James Braid pushed the original concept of the inland landscape to its limits at Gleneagles. In the heart of this land of the "rolling balls" so characteristic of a links, he planned fairways and especially approaches to greens—generally on a larger scale than those elsewhere in Scotland—which force the player to build his strategy chiefly around the "carried ball." The success was immediate.

Braid had preserved a nature less hostile than along the coast. Gleneagles's plateaus, calm waters, and winding hill roads invite the stroller. The player, of course,

takes that walk as he plays a round on one of the four courses united here—the two aristocrats among them being the King's, which is the oldest, and the Queen's, where improvements were recently completed. For once the visual impact cannot be ignored. The vista stretches farther and farther into the distance, toward the mountains of the Highlands through knolls that emerge from a veil of mist. As if to join in the festive spirit, the bunkers tend to slope downhill, offering a clear view of green plateaus whose edges form a plate, a feast of lawn for a party of birdies.

Designed by James Braid shortly before World War I on the interior plateaus of Scotland. King's: opened in 1918, 6471 yards, par 70. Queen's: opened in 1924, 6277 yards, par 70. About 31 miles from Edinburgh.

AUGUSTA

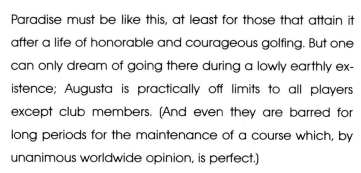

Paradise must be like this, at least for those that attain it after a life of honorable and courageous golfing. But one can only dream of going there during a lowly earthly existence; Augusta is practically off limits to all players except club members. (And even they are barred for long periods for the maintenance of a course which, by unanimous worldwide opinion, is perfect.)

Augusta is certainly not the oldest of golf landscapes. Created in 1933 by a man who had spent a lifetime winning on courses throughout the world, it embodied his dreams of an ideal course, and today it continues to nurture the dreams of others. The man was Bobby Jones, a genius of the game, a practitioner of the highest merit, the only golfer ever to win the Grand Slam. After retiring unbeaten from competition he contacted a Scottish doctor, Alistair McKenzie (the designer of Cypress Point, quite a reference!), to design these eighteen holes. Each year one can return to Augusta and find new marvels. Not that the course has changed from one year to the next; the marvels are always there, waiting to be noticed and appreciated once the spirit has absorbed all the ones discovered before, and the ones discovered before that....

Augusta is a course of absolute classicism, an inland valley dominated by a clubhouse, the tees of the first and tenth holes, and the flags of the ninth and eighteenth holes. The current ninth hole was originally the eighteenth—for one day. After Bobby Jones played his first round on the course he made two decisions: first, he reversed the order of the holes; then he closed the course for a year, though it was already impeccable, to allow it to take, to ripen, to develop. The next year he invited his friends—the best players in the world—and the Masters was born.

With the exception of high rough, which does not exist here but is conveniently replaced by tall trees, there is no golf shot that cannot be played at Augusta. Should a new shot be invented it would no doubt find a place somewhere on this ingenious course where side by side we find valleys, bunkers large and small, bunkerless holes (as on the fourteenth), water traps ranging from the small brook on the thirteenth (comparable to the famous trap on the first hole at Saint Andrews) to the lake on the sixteenth, by way of the ponds on the fifteenth. Added to this are numerous doglegs—not always angled to the left as called for by legend—greens so steep the golfer must putt with his back to the hole (on the fourteenth and sometimes the seventeenth) and so fast they can terrorize even the great lords of the Masters. Everything in this former flower plantation in Georgia, where each hole is named for one of the thousands of blooms, is in such perfect harmony that we remain fascinated, transfixed with admiration. See Augusta, then wait for heaven.

Designed by Bobby Jones and Alistair McKenzie on a former flower nursery and plantation in Georgia. Opened in 1933. 6905 yards, par 72. In the city of Augusta, along the Bobby Jones Expressway.

AQUASANTA

Though golf may be one of the oldest sports on the planet, it seems to be an upstart in this setting: the Via Appia, Rome. An entire empire, one of the birthplaces of civilization, is evoked here on a detour from the paved road, where Caesar's chariot may well have passed.

Today golf carts pass instead. But as if clinging to its setting's history, this Roman course weaves among the vestiges of Italy's most glorious past. Not far away flows the source that later lent its name to this course, Aquasanta—Holy Water. The Romans made extensive use of the water, carrying it to the heart of the Eternal City through a monumental aqueduct, part of which, still standing, crosses the middle of a fairway.

Thanks to the gentle climate of the Roman countryside, the golf course at Aquasanta—more precisely called Circolo del Golf di Roma—is open year-round, with competitions taking place from January through December. Created at the beginning of the century, between 1903 and 1906, this course has been host to some of the most important national and international competitions in Italy. This alone would have extended the course's reputation outside of the Italian borders had the course itself not been sufficient. For it is one of the most beautifully designed inland valley courses in the world. Itself like a grand naturalistic painting with its gentle reliefs, Aquasanta has inspired artists as well. The Scotsman T. Mac Kee—a club member as early as 1906—

captured the gentle undulating countryside in a delicate wash drawing which today adorns the clubhouse where the best of Roman society traditionally mingles until Sunday evening.

Without altering the superb original architecture, modernization allowed the length of the course to be increased to a punishing 6562 yards from the back tees. Despite its length, the Aquasanta course has only two par 5s, one on the front measuring 551 yards—the longest and most difficult hole on the course—the other, far shorter, kicking off the incoming nine at the tenth hole. The outgoing nine of the Circolo del Golf is a more classic par 35 than the final nine, which, while a classic thirty-six strokes, starts with the above-mentioned par 5 followed by its only par 3, a small, extremely graceful

131-yard hole. An uninterrupted succession of par 4s follows (taking the golfer all the way back to the clubhouse) beginning with the most difficult, the 446-yard twelfth hole.

True to its name, the Aquasanta is studded with tiny streams, evidence of the mineral waters that pass through the Roman subsoil. Meandering among the gentle hills of the terrain and coiling around the roots of the numerous pine trees that cast evening shadows, they render this grandiose historic landscape even more hypnotic.

Designed at the beginning of the twentieth century, apparently by local players. The course was opened between 1903 and 1906. 6517 yards, par 71. Seven miles southeast of Rome, near Ciampino.

PORTUGAL
ESTORIL

At first glance this seems a modest course, catering to the leisure of its members as they spend their weekends basking in the sunshine and splendid colors of this residential Lisbon suburb. They seem only to be preparing for the plunge into Portugal's other golf world, that of the Algarve. Situated farther north, facing the Atlantic Ocean, Estoril seems limited by comparison—but only at first!

Admittedly, Estoril's 5698-yard par 69 reminds us that the course was built just after World War II, before the mania for long distances had crossed the Atlantic to the Old World. The progression of the course is even structured around a picturesque imbalance—four par 3s going out, and only one coming in. Estoril seems to try to startle the player out of the lethargy induced by its gentle landscape of pines, mimosas, and rolling hills extending as far as the eye can see: one is quickly surprised by the true difficulty of this inland valley course. It is as if Mackenzie Ross, Estoril's celebrated architect, aimed to include every possible challenge and variation in a minimal space.

Pines shelter the fairways, numerous slopes ward off a false sense of security, and water hazards seem to appear out of nowhere, forcing the player to the heights of his talent. The bunkers that surround every green, with their thick, almost fleshy edges, seem ready to bite by curling around their sandy teeth. On these narrow holes the player quickly forgets—at least for the time it takes to make a shot—the Sintra Mountains watching over his

shoulder on the third hole, or the marvelous view of the Atlantic at the seventeenth. He would be wiser to concentrate on the numerous doglegs which, although sometimes imperceptible to the eye, add up mercilessly on the scorecard. Wiser still, in fact, to fine-tune his game, sharpening the swing like a pencil to draw purer lines and send the ball straight toward its goal: Estoril is unforgiving. Its visible serenity makes for a solemn course, as is often the case in Latin countries, a reflection of the inhabitants and their lifestyle. In the evening the rays of the setting sun creep through the gaps in the trees, cutting the fairways into strips of light and shadow.

Designed by E. Mackenzie Ross in the foothills of the Sintra Mountains. Course created in 1945. 5698 yards, par 69. Located about 2 miles from Cascais, in the resort of Estoril.

MORFONTAINE

Tom Simpson strikes again! The brilliant creations of the British master—responsible for Chantilly and Ravenstein, among others—are unforgettable. Each underscores the genius of a man who incorporated nature into perfect inland courses, whether in plains or valleys. They are unforgettable, too, because they date from the beginning of the twentieth century and, notwithstanding some modifications—which essentially lengthened the courses to compensate for changes in modern equipment—still hold their own next to late-twentieth-century creations. And often up them one.

Tom Simpson had an ideal surface to work with at Morfontaine, and it is one of his masterpieces. To the north of Paris, the course is built on the domain of the Duke of Gramont, a great early benefactor of French golf who was won over by the sport during his visits to Great Britain. The subsoil is sandy, yet it is in the heart of the forest, moors, and heath of the Ile-de-France. Tom Simpson took full advantage of this unique combination, designing an authentic inland course on a links surface which allows the ball to perform according to the ancestral laws of golf.

Although the course at Morfontaine is not excessively long, it is made for drivers. Indeed, the player must always place his shot precisely in the zone imposed by the architect, or he will not be able to play the approach to the green serenely. But this landing zone is often narrow, rimmed with trees and, more dangerous still, with clumps of heather splendid in color but hazard-

ous in their hunger for balls. Responding to the demands of the modern game, Morfontaine was appreciably extended over the last few years. As a result the tees are raised, highlighting the view but further reducing the margin of error on long shots. The key to Morfontaine is its terrain's undulation, whether highly visible—as on the eighth hole with its hilly fairway and downhill second shot—or so subtle as to be unnoticeable, as on the marvelously warped greens around the holes.

A clubhouse tucked away in the lush greenery welcomes prestigious visitors, discreet members, and quiet gatherings. Here the traditional knowledge of golf and its world result from extensive experience on this dream course, a zone protected from all outside intruders.

Designed by Tom Simpson at the end of the 1920s on a sandy terrain of heather. Opened in 1928. 6631 yards, par 70. About 37 miles from Paris.

THE CALIFORNIA-LINKS

The juxtaposition of these two words might come as a surprise, or even provoke a smile. Bear in mind, however, that the links is the simplest form of golf course; nothing must be done to the land other than packing the earth to indicate natural departures and unexpected arrivals. In reality it is the word "California" that is startling in this context. The imagination is strained: links are in the cold, the wind, the rain, and California is a land of sunshine and dry air. But is it really?

Gusty winds and sandy soil are not unique to the northeast of Scotland. All the coastlines in the world have their share, all coastlines are links—they were links even before we thought of building golf courses on them. While architects are limited in the impact they can make on this terrain, so naturally suited to this noble old game, at least they could take on infinite assignments, as coasts are everywhere on the planet.

But what does the word "California" mean here? To create this new landscape, we first had to turn back to the original Scottish links, the model for courses around the world; only then could we dare to graft onto it an architecture springing from the imperialism of the American lawn which took root in California before World War II. This landscape was practically a carbon copy of the Scottish links, with some American liberty and Yankee violence added to make the California-links both am-

biguous and unforgettable. These courses have left a profound impression surpassed only by that left by their Scottish masters.

Not all Scottish courses are links, and links are not always Scottish. The California-links doesn't mix styles; rather, it builds on the original links blueprint. It, too, exists outside of California—though never in Scotland. That said, some of its most obvious examples remain where they were conceived: on the west coast of the United States, along the magical coastline from San Francisco to San Diego with an interruption at the Monterey Peninsula. There, as if roped in by a winding road, Seventeen Mile Drive, are nestled two dazzling examples of this type of golf course. While only a few steps away from one another, they function in two different realms—one, no doubt among the five most exclusive courses in the world, the other the largest public golf course in existence. They are not completely devoid of trees like their Scottish ancestors. In fact they are only slightly related to these predecessors, tied by a common thread of wind and geological construction. The sprays of raging water that often pound the rocks at their edges contrast with the silent stretches—so flat and dismal before their awakening!—of the original links. The grass is more tenacious here, as if the damp sand allows its roots a firmer grip than in any other soil. The shorelines seem sliced by a giant pocketknife, leaving enormous jagged splinters.

The California-links's beauty is that of a painting left rough around the edges and perfectly brushed in the middle. The original links seemed untouchable, almost taboo. In any case, this narrow strip of land left no room for liberties to be taken with it—and we know today that its first, anonymous architects would never have thought of doing so. The California-links, on the other hand, sprawls. Most often, as modern methods dictate, it re-

constitutes the butterfly design in which holes are grouped together in blocks, usually around the clubhouse. The ninth hole usually brings us home again, a concept perfected during the first anti-links revolution of the nineteenth century, that of the inland. And so, decades apart, with miles between them, the landscapes weave their common threads together once again.

One connecting thread above all others follows the long-suffering player across continents and through centuries: the wind. As in the ancient land of the Celts, nothing shields the California-links from it. On this jagged coast where the golf course often overhangs the sea, the gusts of wind give the impression that one could take flight, be swept away like a wisp of straw or the ball itself, to be buried far below where the waves of the Pacific break into spray iridescent in the sunlight. For the sun still shines! Here, the wind is not an unruly visitor, it is at home. Only the cypress trees resist—but at what cost,

tortured by the incessant gales that lash and cut into them. They bend without breaking, but when the wind slackens they still brace themselves in vain, pitiful scapegoats resigned to the next battering.

Such violence unfurled in such a picturesque setting—here is the ambiguity of the California-links, the eye's pleasure thwarted by an uneasy swing. The extreme sophistication of its design and construction, which had time to incorporate modern methods of planning and maintenance, heightens a sense of assembly. Raw and natural, but at the same time complex and ultra-modern, the California links has perhaps—we will never know for sure—succeeded in bringing the golf landscape full circle.

CYPRESS POINT

It's been called the Sistine Chapel of golf. Facing the endless Pacific on the western edge of the continent, Cypress Point wears both its name and its nickname well—a point on an immense map, with cypress trees so twisted and emaciated by the ceaseless wind that they remain bent like petrified skeletons. But the whole forms a symphony of shapes and colors comparable to Renaissance works of art.

Slightly farther below, the ocean pounds itself into sprays so high that a permanent mist remains in the air, sparkling in the sun. Because of this phenomenon, the grass at Cypress Point shines even when it is dry. The

clubhouse that dominates the first slopes is one of the most exclusive in the world, accessible only to its members. There are no exceptions even during international tournaments like the famous Pro-Am created by Bing Crosby, which was originally held at Rancho Santa Fe before establishing itself on this magical Monterey Peninsula in Carmel Bay after the war. The Pro-Am made Cypress Point immediately famous throughout the world, the closed nature of the club only adding to its mystery.

This intrigue was also fed by the eccentricities of the course built by the brilliant Alistair McKenzie, later the architect of Augusta. His virtuosity quickly brought ad-

miration at Cypress Point, but many were surprised by his two consecutive par 5s going out, and even more by the two back-to-back par 3s coming in, the fifteenth and the famous sixteenth. Was it a mistake?

Not at all—unless on the part of the observers. The most famous hole, the sixteenth, doesn't seem like a par 3. It is even considered the most difficult—in any case, the most spectacular—par 3 in the world. It is said that to succeed is the equivalent of a birdie. Others say it is a par 3 and a half.

In fact, the architect didn't plan it as a par 3 at all. At the time, pars were not assigned to holes. Of course, the distance that separates the tee from the green is that of a par 3, especially with the increased distances and improved equipment of today's game. But don't forget that the wind hurls the balls to the left, precisely where the fairway is located. A fairway on the left, on a par 3? Yes. Don't forget, either, that the ball must pass right over an inlet of the Pacific.

This is a heroic par 3 at the very least—and an extremely penalizing one at that. But it is really a type of golf insanity that is to blame. McKenzie never conceived it to be played directly over the water, toward the green; all of his technical descriptions indicate that he intended it as a par 4 with a drive to the left, to be played shrewdly with or against the wind, approaching the flag as best one could with a small chip shot. Today, once one is familiar with the joys of playing at Cypress Point, the challenge lies in attempting this hole as a par 3. But usually this means trying to prove oneself stronger than the course; and we know that in the game of golf this type of arrogance is rarely pardoned.

Designed by Alistair McKenzie on the bare coast of the Monterey Peninsula in California. Opened in 1928. 6536 yards, par 72. Located 146 miles south of San Francisco, on Carmel Bay.

PEBBLE BEACH

More spectacular than difficult? This highly false impression greets the newcomer to Pebble Beach. And the newcomer can hail from anywhere: this absolute gem of a California-links is a public golf course. It is without a doubt, for its genre, one of the most unforgettable trips along the Pacific coast. But the calm is just a trick played by the first few holes. From the first shot on the sixth fairway, when the player emerges from the dunes to confront the Pacific, Pebble Beach reveals its splendor. From here on there is no respite from the dramatic to and fro, the exhausting stop and go between heroic and strategic holes.

The seventh hole, famous for its beauty, is not long—107 yards—but its green is very small (8 yards wide and 22 yards deep) and surrounded by a tight ring of bunkers. Depending upon the direction of the wind, anything from a sand wedge to the longest iron may be called for here. And the eighth is a perfect example of the heroic hole—all or nothing, "death or glory." Nevertheless it does border on being a strategic hole; it leaves the player who misses his drive the possibility of passing through on the left and still attaining the green in three shots. With a good putt, the par is saved. After a good drive, however, all that remains is a 150-yard shot over a Pacific inlet and a bunker—just short of the green—that receives all balls that have been whipped by the wind. The goal is to successfully play one of the game's most difficult shots—44 yards to get off the fairway. The eight holes on the shores of Carmel Bay enjoy a setting unique

to this world, despite numerous attempts at imitation that proved too hasty or simply unsuccessful. The constant wind makes the greens at Pebble Beach among the most difficult and fastest in the United States—naturally, not intentionally as at Augusta.

The eighteenth is certainly the greatest finishing hole in the world. Its superb beauty is entirely natural. The fairway, from the tee to the green, curves its entire length toward the left so that the Pacific Ocean is "in play" throughout this 548-yard par 5, tempting players into the trap of trying to pass directly to the green in two shots. In reality, one never has the impression of playing directly over the water.

The sensation is completely different from that of hitting hard to overcome a lake, a river, a "real" water trap; the ocean is everywhere. One need only follow the line of the fairway. But approaching the brink often startles the player for a moment, costing him one or two strokes. And here, at the last hole, it's impossible to make them up.

Designed by a Californian amateur champion, Jack Neville, between World Wars I and II. Work began in 1928. 6799 yards, par 72. Located 146 miles south of San Francisco on Carmel Bay.

TROIS-ILETS

One day the master architect Robert Trent-Jones took a tour of the Caribbean and returned with two additional contracts to build French golf courses—administratively speaking only, since they were far from the mainland on the French Antilles. Several years later, the courses on the islands of Guadeloupe and Martinique emerged.

The second island apparently offered the American architect a more suitable landscape. Here he was able to incorporate every dimension of his creativity. The eighteen holes of Trois-Ilets sit apart from the hill where the clubhouse presides, invaded by tropical flowers and hanging leaves, and meander between other hills and magnificent shoulders until their sudden descent toward the sea. In the distance, on the limpid water, a sailboat seems to watch over those who, near a green level with the waves, struggle to correctly judge Trent-Jones's slopes. One is tempted to turn the earth over to see what's beneath this picture postcard. The names of the slopes are musical—Pointe-du-Bout, Fort-de-France, Diamant, la Pagerie. . . .

The architect of course worked this raw material into the concepts he has built on throughout the world for over sixty years. Here are white sand bunkers on the lawn, long and intricate as lace, greens, often vast and always steeply sloped, wide fairways, and numerous water traps that one suddenly discovers from high on a hill. Long tees, as well—though Trent-Jones sometimes dispenses with this option in favor of several tiered and spaced departures. He has played with this topography

to create, artificially, one of the most natural California-links landscapes.

From the back tees Trois-Ilets stretches to a length of 6600 yards, but adds up to a mere par 71—there is only one par 5 going out, on the first, probably most difficult hole. This surprising introduction to the course immediately warns of the challenge confronting the player: on this land where the Empress Josephine was born, we are today the plaything of the emperor of the lawn, the great Trent-Jones.

Designed by Robert Trent-Jones on the Trois-Ilets Peninsula in Martinique. Opened in 1976. 6638 yards, par 71. A few miles from Fort-de-France; can be reached by land or sea.

CASA DE CAMPO

"Teeth of the Dog," revealingly, is the name of the Santo Domingo cove which shelters one of the island's two golf courses. It could as easily be rebaptized "Jaws of the Sea," for it is too calm not to be dangerous.

The star architect of the late twentieth century, Pete Dye, discovered a natural violence at Casa de Campo well suited to his creative expression. Rarely has the cunning struggle between the creator of a golf course and the Earth's Creator been so harsh; this hostile landscape of rocks and coral was carved with pickaxe, chisel, and dynamite. Once its limits had been defined the un-

touched nature around it multiplied in lushness, as· if to avenge itself. The holes were formed of earth and compost, sand and *cachaza*, a unique mixture of sugar cane and fertilizer. The course, surgically yanked from the ground, was finally ready, offering a majestic, illusory calm to its players.

Almost everywhere, grass islands abound in a sea of sand. The par 3s—the seventh hole, at 225 yards, which slams right into the sea, or the thirteenth, 175 yards, with a green surrounded on all sides by sand—are terrifying, intoxicating in length. Black clouds often

pass overhead to warn that wind and water will intensify the battle, or perhaps to announce worse, since the island is often subjected to cyclones and tornados. The bunkers penalize, their abrupt slopes plunging toward the sea; the greens, of shapes ranging from stars to clovers, are complex terrains where one's entire game must be reconsidered if one wishes to leave the course at peace with oneself, or at least with the scorecard.

As a true links with a Californian style, Casa de Campo is visibly related to the great Pebble Beach on Carmel Bay. It has, however, more holes directly along the sea—seven all told, certainly one of the world records. This golf course where one must constantly hit long drives and tighten one's precision is almost inhuman: a rabid course with teeth that bite.

Right next door, Pete Dye took advantage of a different terrain to design a course, called the "Links," more Scottish in style. Although inland, it has no trees, offering a startling imitation of a true Scottish links. The proximity of these two unusual courses embodies a remarkable geographic leap.

Designed by Pete Dye in Santo Domingo, on the property of Casa de Campo. Teeth of the Dog: opened in 1972, 6888 yards, par 72. Links: opened in 1977, 6461 yards, par 71.

THE AMERICAN COURSE

History shows the way. But for Americans, the road often led to a cul-de-sac. These brave immigrants had a virgin territory to build on, constructing landscapes already tested elsewhere. While the first American lawns were taking root, their architects could draw on the links, the inland plain and inland valley courses, and most other types of courses as established models. But these had to be adapted and a new indigenous course invented that took centuries of experience and created something new: the American course.

In the beginning it seems that the creators of this

new genre were timid. Often, in fact, they came from Europe—for the large part champions who taught and demonstrated the game in the New World—and didn't know how to approach this old game, nor where to begin to lay out the green theaters of its courses, in this immense land of possibility. So the first designers took refuge in another type of immigration, importing their own landscapes, not daring to break the chain crafted in the Old World two centuries before. The first golf courses they built here are proof enough that the old traditions were respected. Indeed, the oldest golf club in the United States, built in 1888 near New York, was given the magical name of Saint Andrews!

Once this era of allegiance had passed, however,

Americans seemed ready to try anything. With their players already in record books, they began to impose their ideas. The century was only a decade old when the first American-born champion shook up the immigrant masters. Then, on the desert lawns, the new breed of champion was unleashed, and the final chains preventing the march forward of the American game were broken. It took decades to be rid of some of its excesses and recover the true path forward: the veneration that the champions of the 1960s had for the old British tournament, the Open, helped, as did the immense respect that the "golfer of the century," Jack Nicklaus, had for Scottish landscapes just as he was putting on his architect's hat. Yet the American course—an often insane landscape—had not been rejected, simply cured of its growing pains. Some of its extravagances have endured—the excessiveness of certain island fairways, for example (as in the second hole at Pine Valley, where the course allows the player no margin for error since its zones of grass are positioned within a bunker that runs from tee to green). The American course had gone out of bounds, crossing the limits of what a course must ask of a player and what the player is humanly capable of. The inland, which had first set the boundaries of the penalizing and strategic holes, was beaten at its own game. Beauty came to be measured solely in terms of heroism.

Though the masterpiece at Augusta in the early 1930s had already proven that the strategic course would on the whole always be superior to the penalizing course, the American fairyland thrived for three more decades. Improvements in construction techniques—notably in irrigation systems—helped set the tone. A festival of water traps—in front of the greens, for instance, or over large areas—seemed oblivious to the fact that this obstacle is effective only toward the end of the ball's flight. Large tees, which are easier to maintain with modern technology, became common, to the detriment of the multitude of tees which had existed from the game's inception not only to "handicap" the player according to his or her category—amateurs, pros, women, seniors—but, above all, to offer different angles of attack for the same hole. Large flat bunkers flourished for two reasons: they enabled an easier escape and facilitated upkeep, as the mechanized rakes could not navigate steep slopes.

Architects attempted to balance the picture with small, often very steep greens to make for a difficult putt and enhance the value of the chip shot—with dubious success. In the constant effort to accelerate the game and make it easier for clients who had often payed a fortune to have homes located on a certain hole of their club, approaches to the greens were often extremely comfortable, almost greens themselves (this tendency has been rectified in the important tournaments of recent years, even too much so, by allowing small, dense rough to grow right next to the greens, making for an almost impossible shot—yet another illustration of the back and forth between two excesses). The great champions also helped to drive back the limits imposed by the American course. Having no problems with distance, they often tranquilly attacked the greens. Ordinary par 5s no longer existed, even on courses of over

7000 yards. On the final shots these extraordinary drivers had to be put in their place. Here, indeed, they were confronted with almost indecipherable surfaces.

Thus, the American course was reduced to a simple equation, "power + putting." Its creators, playing sorcerer's apprentices, had wanted to direct, rather than respect, the spirit of the age-old game. But despite its flaws, the American course was often an adventure for golf explorers, extraverted and uninhibited, to discover a landscape unimaginable elsewhere. Today the American course enjoys its own golf culture, which, rather than being what remains when all has been forgotten, is a culture that knows not to go too far, after having already tested the outer limits.

TPC STADIUM GOLF COURSE

The great adventure began January 4, 1986, the day Pete Dye's TPC Stadium Golf Course officially opened. Pete Dye is a magical and terrifying name, suggesting staggering lengths, intense cutouts in the earth, deadly bunkers, and immense greens surrounded by water traps lined with vertical railroad ties. TPC stands for Tournament Player Club, a course where the world's masters are invited to put their talents to the test—not to compete with each other, as that would be too easy, but with the course itself as their most ferocious adversary. Finally, a "Stadium" signals a new concept in golf course architecture—one could almost say a new landscape. It is designed to create the view for spectators, using the high hills as vast bleachers above the greens and providing for ultramodern technology: facilities for television equipment, other media, and backup services. The course functions like a baseball or football stadium, but with seats of grass.

The Stadium Course is located a few miles from Palm Springs in the magical, heavenly land—so popular with multimillionaires—of La Quinta, California. Within the confines of the San Bernadino Mountains, in the desert, it is the jet-set suburb of Los Angeles. The area is teeming with golf courses that rival each other for beauty and offer fodder for the covers of glossy magazines. In the heart of the PGA West resort, where the Stadium Course is located, is also a visitor's course de-

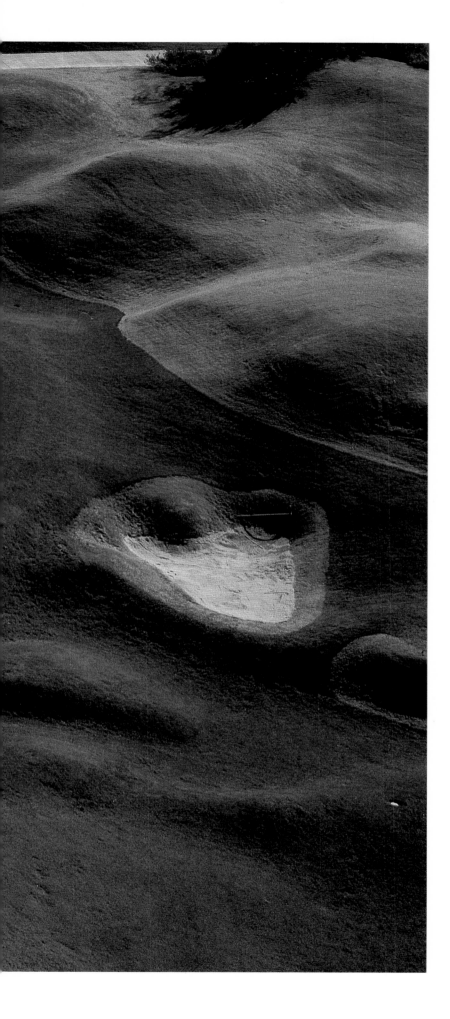

signed by Arnold Palmer, and two others—one a tourist resort, the other extremely private—designed by Jack Nicklaus. But the most famous and spectacular is without a doubt Pete Dye's Stadium Course, featured from its beginning in lists of the world's ten, fifty, and one hundred best courses. Only one figure is necessary to demonstrate its extraordinary difficulty: it is a par 72 but the average scratch sheet score approaches 78 strokes!

In this grandiose space wrested from the desert, an oasis that could advertise the Earth to other planets, the course is a swell of lawn, its waves rolling between bunkers toward greens that are attained only through strength in precision and power. But it is also an honest course—a heavyweight boxer, not a wrestler with underhanded reflexes. It often betrays a bent to the current vogue for double or nothing, the zenith being the infamous seventeenth hole, a par 3 that all of the television stations in the world have focused on, with its green completely surrounded by water. But anything is possible here; it was on this hole, during the most spectacular annual competition in the world, the Skin Games, that Lee Trevino had a hole-in-one.

Designed by Pete Dye in the California desert. Opened in 1986. 7261 yards, par 72. About 20 miles from Palm Springs.

ABIDJAN

Africa is not only a continent but a culture unto itself. With its many races, peoples, and landscapes, it is a world open to our curiosity and wonder. Where golf is concerned, it is as changeable as its landscapes. From the south, which has long enjoyed an Anglo-Saxon golf culture, to the north, which is beginning to open up, by way of the center and the west . . . Yes, the west! Until recently the golf courses found here, usually created by former British colonialists, generally consisted of poorly maintained fairways and greens turned brown. But suddenly, the Ivory Coast revolutionized this old and traditional landscape, and today two large international golf courses can be found here.

One is in Yamoussoukro, the birthplace of Felix Houphouët-Boigny. The second, even more modern and spectacular, is in Abidjan. Though American in size, design, and concept, and of European make (designed with the assistance of the European Golf Consultant), both courses are above all African in their soul and daily life. Here cheerfulness and continual inventiveness exist side by side with luxury and grandiose proportions, and the vast clubhouses are the visitor's first surprise. The Yamoussoukro clubhouse is remarkable due to the soaring lines of Roger Taillibert's vast cupola in pink concrete. That at Abidjan is practically an entire village with its multiple entrances and floors filled with restaurants,

stores, relaxation and exercise rooms, sitting rooms, and balconies overlooking a colorful swimming pool. Not far away, both on the course itself and a few miles down the road, the ultramodern high-rise hotels stand guard like giant sequoias of glass and metal.

With this creation unique to Central and West Africa—enough to make its anglophone neighbors green with envy—Abidjan has established itself on the great international golf circuit. The features of this par 73 course, which stretches for nearly 7300 yards, include three par 5s on the way back in, and a 514-yard finishing hole which, if not the most difficult hole, is spectacular to watch from the terrace of the clubhouse. But what a welcome gift a birdie becomes when one has just played the other seventeen holes—often blocked or rimmed with water and trees so colossal they could house an entire family—which include par 4s that sometimes surpass 460 yards. Here and there within the bunkers tiny patches of grass form minuscule green islands, scale models of the vast, sloping greens to be found at the end of the hole. They remind us of the extreme lushness of African vegetation, of the heat and water that nourish the myriad flowers and fruit trees from which the holes take their names.

Designed by Piero Mancinelli on the outskirts of Abidjan, on the Cocody Peninsula. Opened in 1979. 7277 yards, par 73. On the shores of the Ebrié Lagoon.

MIJAS

Here is Andalusia—the real Andalusia, where the colors of black and ocher form a dancing palette, a silent and secretive land withdrawn from the world. Yet Mijas, one of the great golf courses of the Costa del Sol, is right outside of the noisy, cosmopolitan circuit of its seaside, or rather roadside, neighbors. It's important to venture into the interior of the countryside—a few kilometers are enough—to discover the authentic Andalusia, unchanged for centuries. And the miracle of the course at Mijas is that it does not destroy this authenticity; never incongruous or foreign, it seems to have always been here. Perhaps the clubhouse, an old, almost unaltered Andalusian farmhouse, helps make this fusion so successful. For Mijas is young, both in Andalusian terms and in terms of golf. The first eighteen-hole course here, Los Lagos, was opened in 1976. Los Lagos begins with fanfare, and often with catastrophe. A mere par 71 extending over 6900 yards, it opens with an immense par 5—only a prelude to the two to come, including a colossal fifth hole that surpasses 620 yards! A few holes later, opening the incoming nine, we find a par 4 surpassing 450 yards to tackle.

Even before we scan the first few holes, the extraordinary style of the master American architect, Robert Trent-Jones, becomes apparent. Foothills, water traps, large and twisted bunkers, and ultra-rapid greens studded with thousands of minuscule slopes are enough to unhinge the strongest confidence—if it is not already shaken by numerous mishaps before the final zone.

Trent-Jones's second course, Los Olivos—opened about twelve years later—is slightly narrower and shorter, measuring under 6600 yards for a par 72. But just the same, Trent-Jones couldn't help himself ... Two consecutive par 5s of over 590 yards each, the ninth and tenth, await the player. The finale, typical of the architect's buildup of pressure, is a dramatic progression of a par 3, a par 4, and—the ultimate—a par 5 with a double dogleg.

Right next door, come evening, the recently constructed Byblos Andaluz estate's balconies resonate with the strains of guitar and the guttural voice of a flamenco singer hypnotizing his dancer.

Designed by Robert Trent-Jones in the province of Andalusia, near the picturesque village of Mijas. Los Lagos: opened in 1976, 6942 yards, par 71. Los Olivos: opened in 1984, 6448 yards, par 72. Slightly inland from the Costa del Sol, near Fuengirola.

146

DAR ES SALAM

Africa, whether northern, central, or historically been influenced by its relationship with Europe. But where modern golf is concerned, the influence has been American. The most typical example of this is at Dar es Salam, a few kilometers from Rabat, a course whose breadth has rarely been equaled anywhere in the world.

Golf, however, was not new to Morocco when this crown jewel began construction in the early 1970s. Lawns—first in Marrakech, then in Casablanca (Mohammedia), Fez, Meknes, and Tangier—had been growing for a long time, awaiting the arrival of visitors and residents. The sovereign himself, once initiated to golf, became passionate about this art and wanted to endow his country with a terrain that equaled his ambition and skill. Thus was the idea for Dar es Salam born. Its construction was undertaken shortly thereafter, and with considerable means.

The architect chosen, Robert Trent-Jones, was already at the height of his fame, but had yet to visit the delicate hills of Dar es Salam or observe the vestiges of its thousand-year-old past. He designed three courses together, assigning each one a classic color: red for the most difficult, blue for the one that pretends to be easy, and green for the beginner's course. The lengths establish the hierarchy; the colossal 7464-yard, par 73 course won instant fame with its three par 5s coming in. One of these opens the second half of the course, and another

winds up the traditional, choppy ascension—par 4, par 3, par 5—favored by the American architect.

Aside from its length—which is even more marked going out, with one par 5 surpassing 570 yards and two par 4s extending beyond 440 yards—the course's conception inspired admiration from the beginning. At the time few of these beloved American "monsters" had been seen so close to Europe, with their endless tees, fairways weaving through rows of—fortunately not too rigorous—rough, trees often tightly packed near the approach to the greens, large, white bunkers, tortuous putting surfaces, and irregularly shaped greens cut on the bias to offer an optical illusion or placed on convex basins that repel balls short on backspin. And finally, the water traps! The most famous is on the ninth hole where Trent-Jones, long before most of his current imitators, imagined a true island green. Access is over a small wooden bridge, a new Bridge of Sighs where the player's illusions may fade in a moment.

Designed by Robert Trent-Jones in the southeastern suburb of Rabat on the royal domain of Dar es Salam. Opened December of 1971. Red Course: 7464 yards, par 73; Blue Course: 6786 yards, par 72; Green Course: 2373 yards, par 32.

THE VINTAGE CLUB

A hierarchy of perfection could be established as follows: California is the brightest of the states, Palm Springs is the brightest part of California, and the Vintage fairways are the brightest in Palm Springs. While this may be slightly exaggerated, there is no doubt that it approaches the truth. This unique California spot, like a magical inland extension of Los Angeles, is even more enchanting set in the constellation of towns—La Quinta, Rancho Mirage, Palm Springs, and Indian Wells (where the Vintage Country Club is located)—which shine like stars around it.

Nobody complains about the resemblances between the area's courses, although their holes are nearly interchangeable; the story is often told of a clumsy golfer who drove from the first hole only to realize he had directed his ball to a neighboring course. The fairways are all perfectly straight alongside close-cropped rough. The bunkers are the opposite of sand traps on a links: at times they are vast, at times they serve only to delimit the lawns, and their sands are brilliantly white. The greens are too immense to inspire confidence; to reach them is beyond the grasp of the average golfer, and to read them is always more difficult than it seems under the brutal California sun which, except in the evening when it casts an oblique shadow, barely defines the small slopes.

If the courses seem similar, however, they are hardly identical. Compared to its famous neighbor, the PGA West Stadium, the Vintage Palm Springs seems more

garden than green desert. Trees and shrubs soften the view and lend added color to the typically western ocher on the undulating course. Water is everywhere, as if it were prevented from sinking into a soil so dry that the small rocks at each detour are burning hot. Cacti grow naturally here, evoking the Wild West. The Rocky Mountains form a majestic frame as if to gather the sky's light into this enormous basin where the lawns of new holes and new courses spread outward constantly. And as if to symbolize that the Vintage course, like its surroundings, is more a grown child's dream-come-true than prosaic reality, the electric carts here are even fitted with Rolls Royce radiator grilles.

Designed by Tom Fazio. Mountain Course: 6907 yards, par 72. Desert Course: 6312 yards, par 72. Built in 1979 a few miles from Palm Springs.

DESERT HIGHLANDS

A thousand feet below the lights of Phoenix are aglow. Golfers on their terraces sip long drinks in the cool dusk of the Arizona desert, once the dry heat that bathed their afternoon has faded away. Desert Highlands offers us a postcard-perfect vision, where the smallest house costs a million dollars. Carved into the reddish desert earth of western films, the course is in the highlands, elevated above the urban furnaces of Phoenix and, closer by, Scottsdale. This spot has been known as a center of rural peace since long before the reign of the golf course....

Always on the lookout for new territories, Americans earmarked this one for a new conquest, that of leisure time. Once the industrial fortunes of the great western metropolises had been made, their beneficiaries set about recovering the amenities their ancestors had enjoyed—fresh air, silence, peace, and solitude. Desert Highlands, or at least the idea for it, was born.

The project was quickly completed. Deluxe bungalows, sumptuous villas, shops, private roads, twenty-four-hour guards: in sum, a fabulous resort, a vacation spot with everything—except a golf course. Unthinkable! One of the greatest of modern-day golf course designers, Jack Nicklaus, was brought in. He first visited Desert Highlands in the beginning of the 1980s; during the next two seasons he would be seen there on over twenty oc-

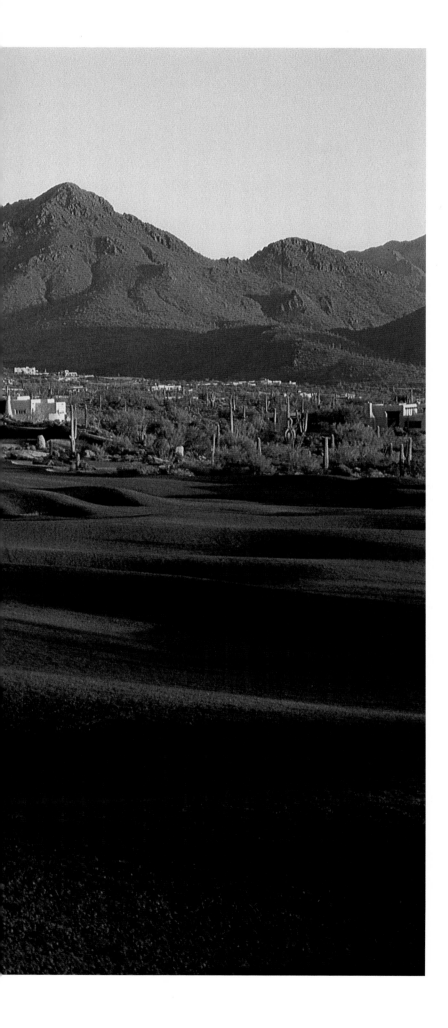

casions, personally overseeing the commission he had accepted. He announced that it would be a top-notch design, one that he would survey himself. Did the golf course architect, a kind of late-twentieth-century adventurer, inherit the original pioneers' love for this land, occupied centuries before by the HoHoKam Indians, and later the Apaches? It's something to ponder while soaking one's feet in the cool water of a pool carved from the jagged rocks by the day heat and the night winds, or upon returning from a tennis match (Desert Highlands is the only complex in Arizona to have every type of surface: clay, concrete, and grass).

Atop the omnipresent sand, Jack Nicklaus sowed some eighty acres of lawn, requiring a prudent irrigation system in this land where water is so rare. His most spectacular architectural theories are united on this par 72, 7099-yard course, constructed in a loop: grass bunkers, undulating mounds, tiny streams, and greens often cut on the bias. Some holes offer as many as seven tees! As dusk falls, a thousand cacti and six hundred aloe veras are silhouetted to complete the picture of this fantastic course, where the first Skin Games were held in 1983 and 1984, and where Nicklaus himself pocketed the most valuable putt in golf history —worth $240,000—on a green he designed himself.

Designed by Jack Nicklaus in the early 1980s. Opened in 1984. 7099 yards, par 72. Located near Scottsdale, Arizona.

THE MOUNTAIN COURSE

Mountain landscapes are not generally suited to golf. The slopes are too steep, the subsoil too rocky, and the weather too harsh. We find neither the sand that makes for good rolling, the sea-level air pressure that impedes the ball's flight, nor the regular winds of the coast. In the mountains the wind blows in swirling gusts rather than sweeping gently, and often too quickly turns into a storm. And yet, over time, the mountain has become a land for

golfers, the result not of the game's natural leanings but rather of its practitioners' enthusiasm as winter sports grew in popularity. The same clientele that played golf in the summer skied in the winter; as winter resorts began to offer amenities to attract summer vacationers as well, golf was added as a further enticement. Everything in these resorts is close by; only the extreme limits of the course feel isolated. Then one returns to friends and family and gets cozy, as if to revel in safety after the steep slopes' adventure. An even stronger factor was a new-found desire to commune with a natural environment that seems untouched—although in reality it is quite developed, having been appropriated without losing any of its mystery.

In the perpetual dialogue that man conducts with himself, a small dot in an immense landscape, there is not much difference between a ski slope and a golf course. At first glance, the mountain course seems reminiscent of the links. Its raw nature, harsh climatic conditions, and strong natural relief may seem to have always been ideal for golf. This, however, is a false impression; the mountain presents a far greater challenge to the golfer than to the skier. If the links is the golfer's paradigm, the mountain course is at the other end of the spectrum. For golf is not only a seaside but a sea-level sport. At the seaside golf benefits from the soil, which is mainly sandy and pure. At sea level, the air density is at its heaviest. It is precisely the lack of sea air and soil that makes the mountain course special.

Here, the steady rhythm of a "normal" course is not possible. This time the course improvises! Nature does not offer the same well-manicured cues it proposes elsewhere, on golf lands destined to be used as such. Yet the mountain course need not be all steep slopes. A mountain may be so vast that its plateaus offer large areas of relatively even ground. These mountain plateau courses take on much the same character as an inland valley, with one important difference. While the architect may shape the course as if it were in a valley, the constraints of the air and soil remain. Rocks puncture the surface, and the oxygen is thin. The mountain course changes all the rules, since it affects both the ball's flight through the air and the way it rolls on the ground.

What remains of the game of golf? Sometimes only the smile of surprise or the powerless rage of the player, who, from his raised tee, discovers the curious bouncing of the ball. It has already flown farther than usual, meaning he should have chosen a different iron, as distances are no longer measured in yards but by the number of the club. And the ball seems to have hit a slanted trampoline. Sometimes the course's improvisation is felicitous and the ball's extra bounce will carry it closer to the green. Sometimes it is ill-fated and the ball becomes one with the thicket, or plunges into a ravine and is lost. Here the game of golf is turned upside-down.

This bouncing-ball scenario no longer occurs at each hole and each stroke. It remains a possibility, but increasingly less frequent due to modern construction, uprooting, and watering techniques. With this problem nearly under control, what remains is the one-on-one with the course, the assessment at face value. But first the rarefied air must be taken into account. At 5000 feet, the difference is always noticeable, and at times spectacular. At this height a player can cover distances that a champion at sea level wouldn't hope for. The steep slopes that mountain courses generally offer are responsible for the highly variable pars for each hole—those par 3s with their greens perched on the side of the mountain against which the ball, just beginning its descent, is brought up short, and the par 5s plunging down into the

valley, the ball falling endlessly and gaining dozens of yards in the process. The mountain course is the only golf landscape on which it is no use to check the scorecard except to verify the sequence of the holes. The mountain

course is an artful liar, with its amusing theatrical somersaults. All around, taller mountains seem to benevolently watch over its antics, proud parents overseeing a mischievous child.

CRANS-SUR-SIERRE

Distance cannot cause isolation on the golf course at Crans-sur-Sierre. As the course is at the heart of the city, golf is in the hearts of its people. They never travel to the course; they are always already there.

The other charm of this eighteen-holer is that of enjoying the same slopes snow-covered in winter, grass-covered in summer. The know-how of the English pioneers who invented the mountain course and its first design at Crans-Montana at the beginning of the twentieth century enabled this astonishing exchange between two great sports which detracts from neither. Later, through prodigious and ingenious invention, considering the constraints of the mountain terrain, the course was modified, pushed back, and today meets international standards, with more than 6800 yards for a par 72. Of course, the 5000-foot altitude modifies the ball's flight. In addition to the known phenomenon of the ballistics of altitudes, variations in levels, downward- and upward-sloping greens—in short, a typical mountain architecture—force the player to adapt constantly. This is one of the pleasures of playing at Crans-sur-Sierre; here is a golf course on which one must be clever! The traditional surprises of bounces and capricious kicks have been eliminated, however, with scrupulous maintenance of the terrain, as well as with its age. All that remains is a heightened dialogue between player and course; an unusual conversation for most of the top pros who have come here to compete each year since the 1939 International Open.

The first hole is a warm-up par 5 of average length. The next few are calmer, until a procession of every possible danger is initiated with the monstrous par 5, 634-yard ninth hole, followed by a long par 4 at the tenth and peaking with the penultimate par 5, the fourteenth, which also surpasses 570 yards. Numerous doglegs heighten the sensation of an aerial voyage, as if the balls were following the flight of the birds, flitting through the pine trees and the rocky peaks, which look on from afar—more than 260 miles of mountains, as far as the eye can see.

A pioneer of adaptation, from a ski town in winter to a town of greens in summer, Crans-sur-Sierre recently sought to further heighten its advantage by asking Jack Nicklaus to design an adjacent course. He created nine splendid holes along the shores of Lake Moubra, measuring 2917 yards, for a par 35. There, too, the colors, the rapidly changing sky, and the yellow flowers scattered against a backdrop of the eternal Alps join in a continual waltz.

Designed by M. Nicholson at the beginning of the twentieth century on the Crans-Montana plateau. Opened in 1907. 6846 yards, par 72. Nicklaus course opened in 1988. At 5000 feet above sea level, in the Valais.

SEEFELD

Upon approaching Seefeld, one immediately senses its density. An all-encompassing landscape, its eighteen holes, considered to be the most spectacular elevated holes in Europe, are concentrated on a few plateaus.

The first, relatively straightforward holes offer a calm and slightly deceptive warm-up, avoiding as they do the steep slopes that encircle this Tyrolean gem. But soon the descent and climb through thick forest intensifies the pervasive sense of density. A typical example is found on the ninth hole, which, though 159 yards long, is approached with a short iron—except when the wind is swirling—as the tee is some 650 feet above the hole! The same phenomenon occurs on the fourteenth hole; despite the enormous 601-yard length of this par 5, two strong shots following the lines of the slope are enough to reach the green. Thus, Seefeld possesses some of the most astonishing holes in Europe. Here the player must always take into account the slopes, inclinations, setbacks—and even water hazards, a rarity on mountain courses!—without forgetting the freer flight of the ball at this altitude.

On this dream mountain course, a fundamental principle of golf strategy—percentages—must be applied rigorously. To calculate the risks is not enough, as there are always risky trajectories, but here more than elsewhere weighing the consequences is the key to success. If it seems easy at first glance, judged only by the small number of bunkers—twenty-seven in all—the mountain course has its own defenses that do not rely on the architect's multiplication of traps which is necessary on flat terrain. The natural doglegs alone are enough, and the choice of a club may require a silent brainstorming session. Indeed, the only sounds here are the rustling of the breeze through the pine trees and, at times, the ricocheting of balls off their trunks. Later, the Tyrolean clubhouse resounds with stories of the course covered in total isolation during the day.

Designed by Donald Harradine on the Wildmoos Plateau in the Tyrol. Opened in 1968. 6709 yards, par 72. Thirty-two miles from Innsbruck.

THE NORDIC COURSE

The Nordic course is the final stop in the golfer's incessant quest for new territories on which to plant his lawn. Nothing beyond it allows for the meeting of man, club in hand, and a topography landscaped to welcome him. Beyond this frontier is nothing but ice-covered lands.

At places like Thorso, Reykjavík, and Skellefteå—names evoking icy mythological spheres—man reached the outer limits. Faced with a horizon that was too white, on these last patches of land where he could still walk without sinking, he decided once again to rework a natural setting, one that could perhaps never be used for anything else. Here he planted the seeds of golf.

In taking this great leap from one barren land to another, at times over thousands of miles, we notice a curious resemblance between the links and its Nordic

descendant. Each borders on an abyss, be it the silent Arctic or the wind-whipped ocean. What could man do, faced with these disturbing deserts? He scratched the earth, removed a few stones here and there, pushed back a little sand, and obtained his response: you can do nothing; turn back. Back a few yards, or a few miles, to return to the first tillable soil. The solid but harsh strip separating the immense desert of ice or water from the nourishing soil had use only as an anteroom. A place to relax, to play, or to collect one's resources for a great encounter: with life and work on one side, or with silence

and death on the other. Only a golf course could find a use for this land. At this northernmost point, it seems that a long drive can reach the end of the Earth.

Those who never tire of conducting an inner discourse are offered a practically uninterrupted solitude by the Nordic course. Near the summer solstice the sun never sets. One can play midnight golf before a solar globe that obliquely skims the horizon, seeming to observe the golfer. It is as if time were standing still, making a gift of itself as at the moment of the Earth's creation. That is how it must have seemed to those who, ages ago, decided to create their course here: a game of frozen light. At lower latitudes nothing can stop the player but darkness. Just as casinos, the temples of gambling, never allow the sun in to betray the passage of time—to satisfy one's passion, the eye must never be forced to adapt and the brain must not sense the passing hours—so on the Nordic course, a temple for golfers, night does not interrupt the player's passion for the game. As long as one can see, one can draw distinctions on the course. It is not that one plays on the Nordic course at night—that could be done elsewhere. It is that night simply doesn't exist. Here one finds a different type of beauty and silence.

The original struggle on this glittering landscape belonged to the architect. For the Nordic course, technique was less useful than a pioneering spirit in a terrain that seemed unvisited by man. Of course, this isn't so, but our predecessors left no traces other than memories covered by trails of lava. Nature practiced a scorched earth policy in these volcanic regions, and it is remarkable that the grass holds fast in spite of everything. Some Nordic courses have been left more or less inaccessible for decades now. The distant exiles who built them never left any indication as to why they struggled to wrest fairways from this hostile land where they must have had more urgent tasks. But however hard man fought to impose his green empire here, he eventually had to surrender. The air is too dry and the land too tough to lend itself to genteel landscaping. Even modern technology cannot erase the excess of snow, of cold, of harsh lighting. On the ground crushed slag, reduced to powder, often replaces the green—a name suddenly out of place! It would be better to call it "brown," as it is defined on the Nordic's southern equivalent, the hot, sandy desert course. And so, in addition to the links, the Nordic has now discovered a new relative, its opposite. Is there much difference? Barren lands resemble one another and are everywhere united.

In the saga of golf, however, it is normal to brandish one's ambition by proffering some blades of grass, which suddenly become enormously symbolic. Even during the war, some British prisoners created ersatz courses in camps where they were held, proof of their immortality through dedication to this green art—against all odds. This same feeling is in evidence on the Nordic course. As proof of his inner warmth man has

taken care to impose wherever he is, in the worst of conditions, his own vision of golf. In lands where there is often nothing to do but wait, he starts the momentum with his clubs, his balls, and his pathetic tufts of grass. And we must salute this instinct for survival.

SKELLEFTEÅ LULEÅ

The name of this club immediately suggests images of sleighs, sliding over an immense icy terrain. True, Skellefteå is a mere 300 miles from the arctic circle, but surprisingly the course does not consist of frozen earth surrounded by icy lakes and traditional red Swedish barns and farmhouses. Quite to the contrary, Skellefteå is a green oasis, inviting the passerby to discover the golf course considered the most northerly on the planet.

This unique setting has two fortunate consequences. During the summer months, the sun never sets! This provides a paradise for golf marathoners; the most lasting memory from a visit to Skellefteå may be to write on one's scorecard, "Tee-off, 1:00 A.M." And because of the perpetual light, the grass never stops growing; the greenskeepers must work almost nonstop, twenty-four hours a day. In the dead of winter, of course, one cannot play a round of golf. The ground, like the water, is frozen, awaiting the warmth of spring and the light of the sun which, once arrived, seems unwilling to detach itself from these eighteen holes, as if surprised to find a course so close by. Even the bunkers give the impression that their lips are chapped.

From the back tees, the course is anything but modest. It easily surpasses the 6700-yard mark, for a classic par 72. At the second hole the player has already embarked on a journey through every angle and distance—the course is on the whole very flat, running through pine trees—encountering time after time what is perhaps the longest water hazard in the world, which

weaves in and out, disappears and reappears throughout the length of the course. This river, the Rönnbäcken, lends its name to the course and silently accompanies the golfer from the first to the eighteenth hole. Through the sunlit day-night Skellefteå offers a powerful sense of being face to face with oneself—what the game of golf is all about.

Designed by Nils Skold and Bo Carlson in northern Sweden, near the arctic circle. Opened in 1970 and 1977. 6709 yards, par 72. A few miles from the city of Skellefteå.

THE HISTORIC COURSE

Was it by chance? Or perhaps the historic course was destined to exist. Of course our terms must be defined: the landscape here, not the golf course set on it, is historic. Were the course historic, it would be elsewhere, nestled in some corner of Scotland—or in Holland, since it was in the Dutch lowlands that this art, which has radiated around the world, originated.

A landscape of historic importance can no doubt be considered independently of its golf course more easily than any other setting on the planet. It may even tend to overpower the landscape—an ancient Egyptian pyramid keeping a silent watch over a humble golf course, barely a century old ... The golfer, in any case, does not separate one from the other. Neither does he separate the Greek columns and the greens of Glyfada, or the aqueduct and the two holes it overlooks at Aquasanta near Rome. The game may not be as influenced by a historic landscape as by an inland valley landscape, or the severe ice of the Nordic course, or the sweeping wind of the links, or the lightness of the mountain course's air. But one may be deeply moved by the landscape nevertheless.

Golf is a game of the mind, where little is needed to tip the scales; the sense that dozens of centuries brood over the player's modern swings weighs heavily enough. And though at first glance the historic course is the most distant from golf's purest function, it is, paradoxically, very close to the game. How? Because it is the only landscape which, like the greens and the fairways it surrounds, is man-made. Landscape and course are embraced as one by the golfer who today uses what his ancestors invented. There is, then, an evident fusion between the game and history, even if the history of the game does not include many memorable pages on the historic course.

Perhaps without realizing it, the golfer feels a great presence around him, and soon within him. The silent and colossal monuments that appear around the bend of a green, or sometimes watch over from the first tee-off to the final hole, point the golfer in a certain direction. Unfortunately, it is not always the one that indicates the best trajectory for his shots! But it is the direction of authenticity; history is kept alive by its concern for truth. The universal epic suggested by the historic course through any of its nearby monuments is on the one hand part of the epic of golf on which the player, like it or not, is bred; on the other hand, it possesses its own inner epic which the game forces him to explore when confronting himself on the course. The history of the world is that of man, and every man carries the history of all others. Thus we can explain our original paradox: the historic course is not a fluke in the history of golf, but rather a necessary step in the story.

MENA HOUSE

We've seen them all but one ... From the original links in the most ancient reaches of Scotland to the American course with its ultramodern facilities—and which we know, despite its sophistication, sometimes resembles the purity of days gone by, when the golf course was only a barely perceptible arrangement of land even sheep passed by—through plain and valley inland courses, California-links, mountain and Nordic courses, we've seen them all but one....

This last course has a setting even older than that of the Dutch shepherds who played a game that is the earliest forebear of golf. The cradle of our civilization, a landscape to revere: the historic landscape. The best example is to be found near Cairo at Mena House. English colonists planted their lawn, at times by force, on this age-old land. But it is not so much the development of the game that we seek at Mena House. It is the past, our own. First there is that nostalgic past of English colonels sporting white, curled mustaches; even the memory of Lawrence of Arabia is still in the air. But dwarfing this, an unfathomable past hovers over the humble greens, worn fairways, and bunkers that are very much at home: the past of the Sphinx, of the Pyramids, of the innumerable deities who seem to guard the most divine creation that man ever made when attempting to imitate the Creator: the golf course.

Designed by an English golf instructor in 1869. Nine fairways and eighteen greens, 6006 yards, par 70. Twenty-four miles from Cairo, near the Giza Pyramids.

SAINT ANDREWS

Links House, Saint Andrews, Fife, KY 169JA
Scotland Tel: (334) 757 57 or 733 93
Golf links, 14 miles (22 km) from Dundee, 50 miles (80 km) from Edinburgh.
18 holes (Old Course). Officially created in 1754.

Hole	Length yds/m	Par	Hole	Length yds/m	Par
1	370/338	4	10	342/313	4
2	411/376	4	11	172/157	3
3	371/339	4	12	316/289	4
4	463/423	4	13	425/389	4
5	564/516	5	14	567/518	5
6	416/380	4	15	413/378	4
7	372/340	4	16	382/349	4
8	178/163	3	17	461/422	4
9	357/326	4	18	354/324	4
	3501/3201	36		3432/3139	36
6933 yds / 6340 m, par 72					

Closed: First two weeks in March, last two weeks in November.
Hotels: Saint Andrews (tel: 334 626 11). Old Course (tel: 334 743 71). Rusack's Marine (tel: 334 743 21).

WATERVILLE

Waterville Golf Club, Waterville, County Kerry
Ireland Tel (667) 41 02 or 41 33
Golf links, 2 miles (3 km) from Waterville, 48 miles (77 km) from Killarney, 109 miles (175 km) from Cork.
18 holes. Created in 1970.

Hole	Length yds/m	Par	Hole	Length yds/m	Par
1	430/384	4	10	476/435	5
2	468/428	4	11	500/457	5
3	439/402	4	12	206/188	3
4	180/165	3	13	517/473	5
5	587/537	5	14	457/418	4
6	374/342	4	15	396/362	4
7	180/165	3	16	366/335	4
8	437/400	4	17	206/188	3
9	440/402	4	18	587/537	5
	3527/3225	35		3711/3393	38
7238 yds / 6618 m, par 73					

Open year-round.
Hotels: Waterville Lake (tel: 667 41 33). Butler Arms (tel: 667 41 44).

MUIRFIELD

Muirfield Golf Club, Muirfield, Gullane, East Lothian
Scotland Tel: (620) 84 21 23
Golf links, 16 miles (25 km) from Edinburgh.
18 holes. Created in 1891.

Hole	Length yds/m	Par	Hole	Length yds/m	Par
1	449/411	4	10	475/434	4
2	349/319	4	11	386/353	4
3	378/346	4	12	381/348	4
4	180/165	3	13	153/140	3
5	558/510	5	14	447/409	4
6	471/431	4	15	396/362	4
7	185/169	3	16	188/172	3
8	444/406	4	17	542/496	5
9	515/471	5	18	447/409	4
	3530/3228	36		3415/3123	35
6946 yds / 6351 m, par 71					

Open year-round (letter of introduction required).
Hotels: Greywalls (tel: 620 84 21 44). Bisset's (tel: 620 84 22 30). Marine (tel: 620 24 06).

BALLYBUNION

Ballybunion Golf Club, County Kerry
Ireland Tel: (68) 271 46
Golf links, 1 mile (1.5 km) from Ballybunion, 174 miles (280 km) from Dublin.
18 holes (New Course). Created in 1977.

Hole	Length yds/m	Par	Hole	Length yds/m	Par
1	437/400	4	10	328/300	4
2	397/363	4	11	142/130	3
3	153/140	3	12	262/240	4
4	404/369	4	13	387/354	4
5	445/407	4	14	398/364	4
6	154/141	3	15	489/447	5
7	346/316	4	16	145/133	3
8	615/562	5	17	484/443	5
9	501/458	5	18	390/357	4
	3451/3156	36		3027/2768	36
6479 yds / 5924 m, par 72					

Open year-round.
Hotels: Marine Hotel (tel: 68 271 39). Central Hotel (tel: 68 271 84).

ROYAL JERSEY

Royal Jersey Golf Club, Grouville, Jersey
Tel: (534) 522 33 or 544 16
Golf links, 4 miles (6.5 km) from Saint-Hélier.
18 holes. Created in 1878.

Hole	Length yds/m	Par	Hole	Length yds/m	Par
1	478/435	5	10	342/313	4
2	143/131	3	11	377/345	4
3	553/506	5	12	388/355	4
4	180/165	3	13	405/370	4
5	369/337	4	14	328/300	4
6	377/345	4	15	191/175	3
7	179/164	4	16	180/165	3
8	129/118	3	17	364/333	4
9	506/463	5	18	322/294	4
	3132/2864	36		2898/2650	34
6030 yds / 5514 m, par 70					

Open year-round.
Hotels: La Plage (tel: 534 234 74). Lavender Villa (tel: 534 549 37). Pomme d'Or (tel: 534 786 44).

LE TOUQUET

Golf Club du Touquet, Avenue du Golf, 62520
Le Touquet-Paris-Plage
France Tel: 21 05 68 47
Golf links, 1 mile (2 km) from Touquet, 62 miles (100 km) from Arras, 93 miles (150 km) from Lille.
18 holes (La Mer). Created in 1930.

Hole	Length yds/m	Par	Hole	Length yds/m	Par
1	514/470	5	10	454/415	4
2	327/299	4	11	420/384	4
3	507/464	5	12	358/327	4
4	502/459	5	13	448/410	4
5	353/323	4	14	500/457	5
6	165/151	3	15	227/208	3
7	381/348	4	16	394/360	4
8	448/410	4	17	188/172	3
9	131/120	3	18	397/363	4
	3329/3044	37		3386/3096	35
6715 yds / 6140 m, par 72					

Open year-round (letter of introduction required).
Hotels: Manoir Hotel (tel: 21 05 20 22). Westminster (tel: 21 05 19 66). Novotel (tel: 21 05 24 00).

TRALEE

Tralee Golf Club, West Barrow, Ardfert Tralee, County Kerry
Ireland Tel: (66) 363 79
Golf links, 8 miles (13 km) from Tralee, 180 miles (290 km) from Dublin.
18 holes. Created in 1986.

Hole	Length yds/m	Par	Hole	Length yds/m	Par
1	396/362	4	10	404/369	4
2	584/534	5	11	571/522	5
3	147/134	3	12	435/398	4
4	423/387	4	13	152/139	3
5	419/383	4	14	384/351	4
6	423/387	4	15	287/262	4
7	141/129	3	16	190/174	3
8	372/340	4	17	344/315	4
9	488/446	5	18	454/415	4
	3392/3102	36		3221/2945	35
6613 yds / 6047 m, par 71					

Open year-round.
Hotels: Mount Bradon (tel: 66 233 33). Ballygarry House (tel: 6o 212 33). Earl of Desmond (tel: 66 212 99).

ROYAL SAINT GEORGE'S

Royal Saint George's Golf Club, Sandwich, Kent
England Tel: (304) 61 30 90
Golf links, 1 mile (1.5 km) from Sandwich, 75 miles (120 km) from London.
18 holes. Created in 1887.

Hole	Length yds/m	Par	Hole	Length yds/m	Par
1	445/407	4	10	399/365	4
2	376/344	4	11	216/198	3
3	214/196	3	12	362/331	4
4	470/430	4	13	443/405	4
5	422/386	4	14	509/465	5
6	156/143	3	15	467/427	4
7	529/484	5	16	165/151	3
8	414/379	4	17	425/389	4
9	387/354	4	18	458/419	4
	3415/3123	35		3445/3150	35
6860 yds / 6273 m, par 70					

Open year-round.
Hotel: Bell (tel: 304 61 33 88).

KILLARNEY

Killarney Golf Club, Mahoney's Point, Killarney, County Kerry
Ireland Tel: (64) 310 34
Inland plain course, 3 miles (5 km) from Killarney, 56 miles (90 km) from Cork.
18 holes (Killeen Course). Created in 1939 (9 holes) and in 1969 (9 holes).

Hole	Length yds/m	Par	Hole	Length yds/m	Par
1	365/334	4	10	170/155	3
2	379/347	4	11	509/465	5
3	196/179	3	12	475/434	4
4	413/378	4	13	442/404	4
5	477/436	5	14	386/353	4
6	195/178	3	15	410/375	4
7	482/441	5	16	497/454	5
8	413/378	4	17	371/339	4
9	382/349	4	18	427/390	4
	3303/3020	36		3684/3369	37
6987 yds / 6389 m, par 73					

Open year-round.
Hotels: Duloe Castle (tel: 64 441 11). Cahernane (tel: 64 318 95). Europe (tel: 64 319 00).

SUNNINGDALE

Sunningdale Golf Club, Ridgemount Road, Sunningdale
Ascot SL 5 9RN, England   Tel (344) 216 81
Inland plain course, 16 miles (25 km) from London.
18 holes (Old Course). Created in 1901.

Hole	Length yds/m	Par	Hole	Length yds/m	Par
1	494/451	5	10	478/436	5
2	484/442	5	11	325/297	4
3	296/270	4	12	451/412	4
4	161/147	3	13	185/169	3
5	410/374	4	14	509/465	5
6	415/379	4	15	226/206	3
7	402/367	4	16	438/400	4
8	192/175	3	17	421/384	4
9	267/244	4	18	432/394	4
	3121/2849	36		3465/3163	36
6586 yds / 6012 m, par 72					

Open year-round.
Hotel: Berystede-Ascot (tel: 344 233 11).

CHANTILLY

Golf de Chantilly, Vineuil-Saint-Firmin, 60500 Chantilly
France   Tel: 44 57 04 43
Inland plain course, 25 miles (40 km) from Paris.
18 holes. Created in 1908.

Hole	Length yds/m	Par	Hole	Length yds/m	Par
1	457/418	4	10	475/434	4
2	396/362	4	11	425/389	4
3	173/158	3	12	402/368	4
4	392/358	4	13	457/418	4
5	434/397	4	14	218/199	3
6	217/198	3	15	417/381	4
7	439/401	4	16	211/193	3
8	576/527	5	17	429/392	4
9	502/459	5	18	596/545	5
	3585/3278	36		3630/3319	35
7215 yds / 6597 m, par 71					

Open year-round (invitation required).
Hotels: Hostellerie du Lys (tel: 44 21 26 19). Château de la Tour
(tel: 44 54 07 39).

GLENEAGLES

Gleneagles Golf Club, Auchterarder Perthshire PH3 1NF
Scotland   Tel: (7646) 35 43
Inland valley course, 31 miles (50 km) from Edinburgh, 16 miles (26 km) from Perth.
18 holes (King's Course). Created in 1918.

Hole	Length yds/m	Par	Hole	Length yds/m	Par
1	362/330	4	10	447/411	4
2	405/371	4	11	230/212	3
3	374/342	4	12	395/364	4
4	466/425	4	13	448/412	4
5	161/152	3	14	260/243	4
6	476/435	5	15	459/420	4
7	439/392	4	16	135/123	3
8	158/155	3	17	377/341	4
9	354/323	4	18	525/485	5
	3195/2925	35		3276/3011	35
6471 yds / 5936 m, par 70					

Open year-round.
Hotel: The Gleneagles Hotel (tel: 7646 22 31).

WENTWORTH

Wentworth Club, Wentworth Drive, Virginia Waters Surrey, GU254LF
England   Tel: (344) 84 22 01.
Inland plain course, west of London, approximately 30 minutes from
Heathrow International Airport.
18 holes (West Course). Created in 1939.

Hole	Length yds/m	Par	Hole	Length yds/m	Par
1	471/430	4	10	186/170	3
2	155/141	3	11	376/343	4
3	452/413	4	12	483/441	5
4	501/457	5	13	441/403	4
5	191/174	3	14	179/163	3
6	344/314	4	15	466/425	4
7	399/364	4	16	380/347	4
8	398/363	4	17	571/521	5
9	450/411	4	18	502/458	5
	3361/3067	35		3584/3271	37
6945 yds / 6338 m, par 72					

Open year-round.
Hotel: Berystede-Ascot (tel: 344 233 11).

BREMEN ZUR VAHR

Bremen zur Vahr, Bürg Spitta, Allee 34, Bremen
Germany   Tel: (421) 23 00 41
Inland plain course, 5 miles (8 km) from Bremen.
18 holes. Created in 1963 (9 holes in 1905).

Hole	Length yds/m	Par	Hole	Length yds/m	Par
1	355/325	4	10	547/500	5
2	536/490	5	11	191/175	3
3	208/190	3	12	509/465	5
4	569/520	5	13	421/385	4
5	334/305	4	14	355/325	4
6	574/525	5	15	558/510	5
7	410/375	4	16	454/415	4
8	170/155	3	17	230/210	3
9	427/390	4	18	416/380	4
	3582/3275	37		3680/3365	37
7262 yds / 6640 m, par 74					

Open year-round.
Hotel: Strandlust (tel: 421 66 60 63).

AUGUSTA

Augusta National Golf Club, P.O. Box 2086, Augusta,
Georgia 30913
Tel: (404) 738-7761
Inland valley course, in Augusta, 65 miles from Columbia, South Carolina, 71 miles from Atlanta, Georgia.
18 holes. Created in 1931.

Hole	Length yds/m	Par	Hole	Length yds/m	Par
1	400/366	4	10	485/443	4
2	555/507	5	11	455/416	4
3	360/329	4	12	155/142	3
4	205/187	3	13	465/425	5
5	435/398	4	14	405/370	4
6	180/165	3	15	500/457	5
7	360/329	4	16	170/155	3
8	535/489	5	17	400/366	4
9	435/398	4	18	405/370	4
	3465/3168	36		3440/3144	36
6905 yds / 6312 m, par 72					

Open from October to May (invitation required).
Hotel: Ramada Inn (tel: 904 736-2595).

LES BORDES

Les Bordes, 41220 Saint-Laurent-Nouan
France   Tel: 54 84 72 13
Inland plain course, 16 miles (25 km) from Orléans, 99 miles (160 km) from Paris.
18 holes. Created in 1987.

Hole	Length yds/m	Par	Hole	Length yds/m	Par
1	439/401	4	10	512/468	5
2	522/477	5	11	402/368	4
3	388/355	4	12	413/378	4
4	165/151	3	13	185/169	3
5	435/398	4	14	558/510	5
6	385/352	4	15	437/400	4
7	507/464	5	16	215/197	3
8	156/143	3	17	454/415	4
9	390/357	4	18	447/409	4
	3388/3098	36		3624/3314	36
7012 yds / 6412 m, par 72					

Open year-round.
Hotels: Les Bordes (tel: 54 87 72 13). L'Abbaye (tel: 38 44 67 35).
La Tonnellerie (tel: 38 44 68 15).

RAVENSTEIN

Royal Belgique, Château de Ravenstein, 1980 Tervuren
Belgium   Tel: (2) 767 58 01
Inland plain course, 6 miles (10 km) from Brussels.
18 holes. Created in 1906.

Hole	Length yds/m	Par	Hole	Length yds/m	Par
1	491/449	5	10	349/319	4
2	420/384	4	11	417/381	4
3	156/143	3	12	194/177	3
4	414/379	4	13	523/478	5
5	511/467	5	14	325/297	4
6	209/191	3	15	514/470	5
7	373/341	4	16	336/307	4
8	361/330	4	17	419/383	4
9	336/307	4	18	305/279	4
	3271/2991	36		3380/3091	37
6651 yds / 6082 m, par 73					

Open year-round.
Hotel: Park Hotel (tel: 2 736 32 10).

AQUASANTA

Aquasanta Golf Club, Via dell'Aquasanta N 3
Via Appia Nuova 716/A, 00178 Rome
Italy   Tel: (99) 643 92 51
Inland valley course, 4 miles (7 km) from Rome.
18 holes. Created in 1903.

Hole	Length yds/m	Par	Hole	Length yds/m	Par
1	355/325	4	10	341/312	4
2	189/173	3	11	412/377	4
3	562/514	5	12	565/517	5
4	408/373	4	13	162/148	3
5	350/320	4	14	372/340	4
6	388/355	4	15	195/178	3
7	223/204	3	16	524/479	5
8	433/396	4	17	399/365	4
9	337/308	4	18	302/276	4
	3246/2968	35		3272/2992	36
6518 yds / 5960 m, par 71					

Open year-round.
Hotels: Golf Hotel (tel: 99 643 92 51). Villa Giusy (tel: 99 643 30 36).

ESTORIL

Clubo de Golf do Estoril, Av. dos Bombeiros Voluntarios
2765 Estoril, Portugal   Tel: (1) 268 13 76
Inland valley course, 2 miles (3 km) from Cascais, 6 miles (10 km) from Lisbon.
18 holes. Created in 1945.

Hole	Length yds/m	Par	Hole	Length yds/m	Par
1	385/352	4	10	386/353	4
2	156/143	3	11	506/463	5
3	319/292	4	12	420/384	4
4	171/156	3	13	273/250	4
5	517/473	5	14	396/362	4
6	266/243	4	15	326/298	4
7	419/383	4	16	215/197	3
8	215/197	3	17	282/258	4
9	171/156	3	18	273/250	4
	2619/2395	33		3079/2815	33

5698 yds / 5210 m, par 69

Open year-round.
Hotels: Estoril Palacio Luxe (tel: 1 268 04 00). Atlantico, Monte Estoril (tel: 1 268 02 70).

PEBBLE BEACH

Pebble Beach Golf Links, P.O. Box 658, Pebble Beach, California, 93953
Tel: (408) 624-3811
California-links course, 146 miles from San Francisco, 2.5 miles from Carmel, 3 miles from Monterey.
18 holes. Created in 1919.

Hole	Length yds/m	Par	Hole	Length yds/m	Par
1	373/341	4	10	426/390	4
2	502/459	5	11	384/351	4
3	388/355	4	12	202/185	3
4	327/299	4	13	392/358	4
5	166/152	3	14	565/517	5
6	516/472	5	15	397/363	4
7	107/98	3	16	402/368	4
8	431/394	4	17	209/191	3
9	464/424	4	18	548/501	5
	3274/2994	36		3525/3224	36

6799 yds / 6218 m, par 72

Open year-round.
Hotels: Carmel Valley Ranch Resort (tel: 408 626-9500). Spanish Bay (tel: 408 647-7500). La Playa (tel: 408 624-6476).

TPC STADIUM GOLF COURSE

PGA West, 56-150 PGA Boulevard, La Quinta, California 92253
Tel: (619) 564-7429
American course, 10 miles from Rancho Mirage, 15 miles from Palm Springs, 121 miles from Los Angeles.
18 holes. Created in 1986.

Hole	Length yds/m	Par	Hole	Length yds/m	Par
1	440/402	4	10	414/378	4
2	373/341	4	11	618/565	5
3	470/430	4	12	360/329	4
4	184/168	3	13	220/201	3
5	533/487	5	14	390/357	4
6	255/233	3	15	470/430	4
7	350/320	4	16	571/522	5
8	557/509	5	17	166/152	3
9	450/411	4	18	440/402	4
	3612/3301	36		3649/3336	36

7261 yds / 6637 m, par 72

Open year-round.
Hotels: La Quinta (tel: 619 564-4111). Hyatt (tel: 619 321-1940).

MORFONTAINE

Golf de Morfontaine, 60128 Mortefontaine
France   Tel: 44 54 68 27
Inland valley course, 7.5 miles (12 km) from Senlis, 28 miles (45 km) from Paris.
18 holes. Created in 1928.

Hole	Length yds/m	Par	Hole	Length yds/m	Par
1	475/434	4	10	374/342	4
2	220/201	3	11	167/153	3
3	478/437	5	12	522/477	5
4	195/178	3	13	162/148	3
5	361/330	4	14	383/350	4
6	405/370	4	15	459/420	4
7	440/402	4	16	475/434	4
8	437/400	4	17	184/168	3
9	389/356	4	18	506/463	5
	3399/3108	35		3232/2955	35

6631 yds / 6063 m, par 70

Open year-round (invitation required).
Hotels: Croix d'Or (tel: 44 54 00 04). Hostellerie de la Porte Bellon (tel: 44 53 03 05). Le Relais d'Aumale (tel: 44 54 61 31).

TROIS-ILETS

Golf Country Club de la Martinique, 97229 Trois-ilets
Martinique F.W.I.   Tel: (596) 68 32 81
California-links course, 9 miles (15 km) from Lamentin, 12.5 miles (20 km) from Fort-de-France.
18 holes. Created in 1976.

Hole	Length yds/m	Par	Hole	Length yds/m	Par
1	515/471	5	10	390/357	4
2	370/338	4	11	210/192	3
3	200/183	3	12	540/494	5
4	420/384	4	13	395/361	4
5	340/311	4	14	505/462	5
6	389/356	4	15	195/178	3
7	175/160	3	16	490/448	5
8	360/329	4	17	245/224	3
9	459/420	4	18	440/402	4
	3228/2952	35		3410/3118	36

6638 yds / 6070 m, par 71

Open year-round.
Hotel: Meridien (tel: 596 73 60 00).

PGA WEST—JACK NICKLAUS RESORT

Address same as above.
18 holes. Created in 1988.

Hole	Length yds/m	Par	Hole	Length yds/m	Par
1	401/367	4	10	364/333	4
2	440/402	4	11	525/480	5
3	187/171	3	12	182/166	3
4	542/496	5	13	417/381	4
5	357/326	4	14	435/398	4
6	457/418	4	15	561/513	5
7	520/475	5	16	436/399	4
8	164/150	3	17	210/192	3
9	470/430	4	18	458/419	4
	3538/3235	36		3588/3281	36

7126 yds / 6516 m, par 72

CYPRESS POINT

Cypress Point Club, Pebble Beach, P.O. Box 466, California 93953
Tel: (408) 624-6444
California-links course, 146 miles from San Francisco, 3 miles from Monterey.
18 holes. Created in 1928.

Hole	Length yds/m	Par	Hole	Length yds/m	Par
1	421/382	4	10	480/449	5
2	458/504	5	11	437/397	4
3	162/147	3	12	404/374	4
4	384/352	4	13	365/331	4
5	493/449	5	14	388/350	4
6	518/477	5	15	143/127	3
7	168/149	3	16	231/213	3
8	363/325	4	17	393/344	4
9	292/266	4	18	346/313	4
	3349/3051	37		3187/2898	35

6536 yds / 5949 m, par 72

Open year-round.
Hotels: The Lodge (tel: 408 624-3811). Spanish Bay (tel: 408 647-7500). Monterey Plaza (tel: 408 646-1700).

CASA DE CAMPO

Casa de Campo, La Romana
Dominican Republic   Tel: (809) 523 3333
California-links course, 1½ hours from Santo Domingo.
18 holes (Teeth of the Dog). Created in 1974.

Hole	Length yds/m	Par	Hole	Length yds/m	Par
1	401/367	4	10	377/345	4
2	377/345	4	11	540/494	5
3	545/498	5	12	445/407	4
4	327/299	4	13	175/160	3
5	155/142	3	14	505/462	5
6	448/410	4	15	384/351	4
7	225/206	3	16	185/169	3
8	417/381	4	17	435/398	4
9	505/462	5	18	440/402	4
	3401/3110	36		3486/3188	36

6888 yds / 6298 m, par 72

Open year-round.
Hotel: La Romana (tel: 809 523 3333).

ABIDJAN

Ivoire Golf Club, 08 - BP 01 - Abidjan 08
Ivory Coast   Tel: 43 08 45
American course, 15.5 miles (25 km) from the Abidjan/Port-Bouët International Airport, 28 miles (45 km) from Bassan, 186 miles (300 km) from Yamoussoukro.
18 holes. Created in 1979.

Hole	Length yds/m	Par	Hole	Length yds/m	Par
1	423/387	4	10	423/387	4
2	431/394	4	11	175/160	3
3	527/482	5	12	509/465	5
4	413/378	4	13	344/315	4
5	443/405	4	14	574/525	5
6	190/174	3	15	386/353	4
7	464/424	4	16	175/160	3
8	201/184	3	17	463/423	4
9	571/522	5	18	514/470	5
	3664/3350	36		3613/3304	37

7277 yds / 6654 m, par 73

Open year-round.
Hotels: Hotel Ivoire Golf (tel: 44 10 45). Hotel du Golf (tel: 43 10 44).

MIJAS

Campo de Golf de Mijas, Aparto 138, Fuengirola
Spain Tel: (52) 47 68 43
American course, 18.5 miles (30 km) from Marbella, 17 miles (28 km) from Malaga.
18 holes (Los Lagos). Created in 1976.

Hole	Length yds/m	Par	Hole	Length yds/m	Par
1	573/524	5	10	451/412	4
2	173/158	3	11	197/180	3
3	375/343	4	12	382/349	4
4	429/392	4	13	577/528	5
5	624/571	5	14	365/334	4
6	428/391	4	15	183/167	3
7	419/383	4	16	405/370	4
8	225/206	3	17	378/346	4
9	390/357	4	18	369/337	4
	3636/3325	36		3306/3023	35

6942 yds / 6348 m, par 71

Open year-round.
Hotel: Byblos Andaluz (tel: 52 47 68 43).

THE VINTAGE CLUB—DESERT COURSE

Address same as above.
18 holes. Created in 1980.

Hole	Length yds/m	Par	Hole	Length yds/m	Par
1	376/344	4	10	374/342	4
2	429/392	4	11	288/263	4
3	301/275	4	12	517/473	5
4	501/458	5	13	399/365	4
5	208/190	3	14	197/180	3
6	510/466	5	15	308/282	4
7	157/144	3	16	147/134	3
8	350/320	4	17	470/430	4
9	410/375	4	18	370/338	4
	3242/2964	36		3070/2807	36

6312 yds / 5772 m, par 72

SEEFELD

Golf Club Seefeld-Wildmoos, A-6100 Seefeld, Postfach 22
Austria Tel: (5212) 30 03 or 23 13
Mountain course, 2.5 miles (4 km) from Seefeld, 12 miles (20 km) from Innsbruck.
18 holes. Created in 1968.

Hole	Length yds/m	Par	Hole	Length yds/m	Par
1	519/475	5	10	405/370	4
2	437/400	4	11	317/290	4
3	328/300	4	12	569/520	5
4	388/355	4	13	180/165	3
5	246/225	3	14	601/550	5
6	388/355	4	15	416/380	4
7	574/525	5	16	339/310	4
8	284/260	4	17	186/170	3
9	159/145	3	18	372/340	4
	3325/3040	36		3385/3095	36

6709 yds / 6135 m, par 72

Open from May to October.
Hotels: Astoria (tel: 5212 22 72). Prachenskyhof (tel: 5212 27 22). Klausterbräu (tel: 5212 26 21).

DAR ES SALAM

Royal Golf Club de Dar es Salam, Route de Zaiers, Rabat
Morocco Tel: (7) 7558 64
American course, 7.5 miles (12 km) from Rabat.
18 holes (Red Course). Created in 1971.

Hole	Length yds/m	Par	Hole	Length yds/m	Par
1	409/374	4	10	483/442	5
2	233/213	3	11	464/424	4
3	454/415	4	12	569/520	5
4	424/388	4	13	389/356	4
5	569/520	5	14	210/192	3
6	443/405	4	15	396/362	4
7	430/393	4	16	430/393	4
8	574/525	5	17	225/206	3
9	199/182	3	18	563/515	5
	3735/3415	36		3729/3410	37

7464 yds / 6825 m, par 73

Open year-round.
Hotels: Hyatt Regency (tel: 7 7712 34). Tour Hassan (tel: 7 7214 01).

DESERT HIGHLANDS

Desert Highlands Golf Club, 10040 East Happy Valley Road,
Scottsdale, Arizona 85255 Tel: (602) 861-0305
American course, 34 miles from Phoenix.
18 holes. Created in 1984.

Hole	Length yds/m	Par	Hole	Length yds/m	Par
1	356/326	4	10	408/373	4
2	584/534	5	11	564/516	5
3	452/413	4	12	177/162	3
4	211/193	3	13	396/362	4
5	425/389	4	14	417/381	4
6	431/394	4	15	145/133	3
7	190/174	3	16	244/223	3
8	438/401	4	17	570/521	5
9	567/518	5	18	524/479	5
	3654/3342	36		3445/3150	36

7099 yds / 6492 m, par 72

Open year-round.
Hotels: Princess Resort (tel: 602 585-4848). Hyatt Regency (tel: 602 991-3388).

SKELLEFTEÅ LULEÅ

Skellefteå Golf Club, Box 152,931 22 Skellefteå 1
Sweden Tel: (910) 793 33 or 156 04
18 holes. Created in 1968.

Hole	Length yds/m	Par	Hole	Length yds/m	Par
1	352/322	4	10	566/518	5
2	547/500	5	11	414/379	4
3	375/343	4	12	409/374	4
4	203/186	3	13	168/154	3
5	504/461	5	14	383/350	4
6	355/325	4	15	138/126	3
7	175/160	3	16	604/552	5
8	383/350	4	17	361/330	4
9	384/351	4	18	387/354	4
	3279/2998	36		3431/3137	36

6709 yds / 6135 m, par 72

Open from May to October.
Hotels: Malmia (tel: 910 773 00). Stads (tel: 910 141 40).

THE VINTAGE CLUB—MOUNTAIN COURSE

The Vintage Club, 75001 Fairway Drive, Indian Wells
California 92260 Tel: (619) 340-0500
American course, 20 miles from Palm Springs, 118 miles from Los Angeles.
18 holes. Created in 1980.

Hole	Length yds/m	Par	Hole	Length yds/m	Par
1	414/379	4	10	411/376	4
2	418/382	4	11	185/169	3
3	448/410	4	12	412/377	4
4	409/369	4	13	316/289	4
5	204/187	3	14	440/402	4
6	609/557	5	15	526/481	5
7	166/152	3	16	406/371	4
8	349/319	4	17	144/132	3
9	552/505	5	18	503/460	5
	3564/3260	36		3343/3057	36

6907 yds / 6317 m, par 72

Open year-round.
Hotels: La Quinta Hotel (tel: 619 546-4111). Howard Johnson Hotel (tel: 619 340-4303).

CRANS-SUR-SIERRE

Golf Club de Crans-sur-Sierre, 3963 Crans-sur-Sierre
Switzerland Tel: (27) 41 21 68
Mountain course, 9 miles (15 km) from Sierre, 112 miles (180 km) from Geneva.
18 holes. Created in 1907.

Hole	Length yds/m	Par	Hole	Length yds/m	Par
1	519/475	5	10	405/370	4
2	432/395	4	11	213/195	3
3	186/170	3	12	399/365	4
4	503/460	5	13	208/190	3
5	355/325	4	14	574/525	5
6	328/300	4	15	514/470	5
7	317/290	4	16	328/300	4
8	191/175	3	17	355/325	4
9	634/580	5	18	383/350	4
	3467/3170	36		3379/3090	36

6846 yds / 6260 m, par 72

Open from May to October.
Hotels: Hôtel du Golf (tel: 27 41 42 42). Grand Hôtel Rhodania (tel: 27 40 11 41).

MENA HOUSE

Route des Pyramides, Giza, Cairo
Egypt Tel: (2) 38 75 583
Historic course, 10 miles (16 km) from Cairo, 3 hours from Alexandria.
18 holes (9 fairways, 18 greens). Created in 1971.

Hole	Length yds/m	Par	Hole	Length yds/m	Par
1	455/416	5	10	455/416	5
2	155/142	3	11	155/142	3
3	390/357	4	12	390/357	4
4	364/333	4	13	364/333	4
5	216/198	3	14	216/198	3
6	213/195	3	15	213/195	3
7	350/320	4	16	350/320	4
8	345/315	4	17	345/315	4
9	515/471	5	18	515/471	5
	3003/2746	35		3003/2746	35

5492 yds / 6006 m, par 70

Open year-round.
Hotel: Mena House Oberoi (tel: 2 85 79 99).

LIST OF ILLUSTRATIONS